POLYMER CLAY
MIXED MEDIA
Jewelry

Shirley Rufener

POLYMER CLAY
MIXED MEDIA
Jewelry

fresh
techniques,
projects
and
inspiration

Shirley Rufener

kp

CINCINNATI, OHIO

mycraftivity.com
connect. create. explore.

fw *media*

Other fine Krause Publications titles are available from your local bookstore, craft supply store, online retailer or visit our website at www.fwmedia.com.

13 12 11 10 09   5 4 3 2 1

DISTRIBUTED IN CANADA BY FRASER DIRECT
100 Armstrong Avenue
Georgetown, ON, Canada L7G 5S4
Tel: (905) 877-4411

DISTRIBUTED IN THE U.K. AND EUROPE BY DAVID & CHARLES
Brunel House, Newton Abbot, Devon, TQ12 4PU, England
Tel: (+44) 1626 323200, Fax: (+44) 1626 323319
Email: postmaster@davidandcharles.co.uk

DISTRIBUTED IN AUSTRALIA BY CAPRICORN LINK
P.O. Box 704, S. Windsor NSW, 2756 Australia
Tel: (02) 4577-3555

Library of Congress Cataloging-in-Publication Data
Rufener, Shirley.
  Polymer clay mixed media jewelry / by Shirley Rufener. – 1st ed.
      p. cm.
  ISBN 978-0-89689-689-5
  1. Polymer clay craft. 2. Jewelry making. I. Title.
  TT297.R94 2009
  745.57'2–dc22
                              2008044735

Edited by Vanessa Lyman
Cover designed by Nicole Armstrong
Designed by Kristina Rolander
Production coordinated by Matt Wagner
Step-by-step photography by Shirley Rufener
All other photography by Ric Deliantoni, unless otherwise noted.

ABOUT THE AUTHOR

Shirley Rufener is a designer and TV demonstrator. She has regularly contributed to a range of publications, including creative craft booklets and craft magazines. Shirley has appeared on national TV broadcasts including "The Carol Duvall Show," "The Creative Life" on PBS Plus and the "Home Shopping Network." For the past eight years Shirley has been the craft expert on a popular morning show in Portland, Oregon. These monthly TV demonstrations have shown viewers how easy it can be to make your own fashion accessories, home décor items and gifts. Shirley has also taught polymer clay and various mixed media workshops for several years. She is a certified professional demonstrator (CPD) with the Craft & Hobby Association (CHA) and has demonstrated various art and craft products for manufacturers at craft stores, chain stores, scrapbook shops and trade shows. Shirley currently resides on the beautiful Oregon coast with her husband Dwayne, the love of her life. She is the mother of two very talented grown children, Joy and Daniel.

METRIC CONVERSION CHART

TO CONVERT	TO	MULTIPLY BY
Inches	Centimeters	2.54
Centimeters	Inches	0.4
Feet	Centimeters	30.5
Centimeters	Feet	0.03
Yards	Meters	0.9
Meters	Yards	1.1

Dedication

I dedicate this book to Dwayne, my husband, whose encourage- ment and willingness to help me with whatever crazy thing I ask of him made this book possible. He has constantly cheered me on in all my endeavors, saying, "I know you can do it!" Thanks, honey, for being there for me every step of the way, for all you do for me and for your constant love.

TABLE OF CONTENTS

INTRODUCTION

Polymer clay is one of the most exciting mediums available to work with. There are so many aspects yet to be discovered that the possibilities seem endless. It can be molded into any shape, it is fabulous at imitating other materials and you really can't make a mistake that can't be fixed. As long as you haven't baked your piece yet, if you don't like what you've made, simply roll it back into a ball and start over. What medium could be as forgiving as that?

Within this book, you will find fresh polymer clay techniques, as well as some new twists on a few older ones. While the projects are aimed at beginners to intermediate crafters, my hope is that accomplished artists in this medium will enjoy trying some new techniques and mixed media applications that will, in turn, provide inspiration for their work. There are a wide variety of styles and projects to choose from, each containing mixed media applications. I have tried to include a variety of jewelry styles in the hope that something will catch the eye of a very diverse group of readers, crafters and artists. My jewelry may not be as edgy as some artists, but I am confident that I have presented truly wearable pieces that will appeal to others like myself. I have also included a gallery of "eye candy" in the gallery section. I am thrilled and so privileged to be able to share a variety of jewelry pieces created by many of the leading polymer clay artists around the country, as well as internationally. My hope is that the work will inspire you and show you just how versatile this medium really is.

Over the past several years as the "craft expert" on a popular TV morning show, I have demonstrated a huge variety of crafts. But when it comes to my hobby and my free time, I always head to my favorite medium in my studio, my polymer clay. It is the only art medium that I have consistently worked with for the past twenty years. I love being able to mold something with my own two hands and then make it permanent in an oven. And it is so much fun to wear "matching" jewelry and see the reactions I get from people who think I must have spent hours shopping for that perfect accessory for my outfit.

My goal for you is that as you browse through the jewelry in this book, you will catch the polymer clay bug. I hope you will get as excited as I am as you create your own fabulous jewelry. Let your style come through as you choose colors that you like to wear and designs that fit your lifestyle and personality. Jewelry is personal adornment, so make it your own. My materials lists contain clay colors that I have used on the sample projects. I encourage you to choose colors that you like and think would look good on a specific project. Allow my suggestions to become jumping-off points for you. Learn the techniques and then change them up. Experiment! Add embellishments that you prefer, and create jewelry that you like to wear.

Allow yourself to unleash the creativity inside. I believe that everyone is creative—you just have to take the time to find your niche. Part of that includes giving something a shot that you haven't tried before. More importantly, allow yourself time to get the hang of it. Don't expect perfection on your first or even second or third attempt at working with polymer clay. It is a learned art that I know you can accomplish.

When teaching polymer clay workshops, I actually prefer using the term "playing with clay" as opposed to "working with clay" because for me, it is just so much fun! I encourage everyone to have a hobby of some type. No matter what your age, you still need to stop and take time to play.

SECTION ONE

Getting Started

Everything in this section is geared toward those of you who are just starting to work with polymer clay, although intermediate and even experienced clay artists may find a few new tools or techniques to try. You'll discover that the tools you use the most are your hands. They provide warmth to the clay, which makes it soft enough to condition, plus, you don't have to go searching for them in your toolbox. If you ever had the chance to play with salt dough or kid's clay as a child, then you know how much fun it is to squish it between your fingers and mold it into whatever you could imagine. Polymer clay is a lot like that, but once you're satisfied with your work, you can bake it to make it hard... on purpose!

WORKING WITH POLYMER CLAY

Polymer clay is a man-made modeling material. For the sake of this book, we will call it "clay," as it is a malleable material that can be worked like clay. It's different from earth clays because the compound is pre-colored for you. You can use purchased colors and mix them into any color you can imagine. It's available in opaque colors, translucents and metallics that give a beautiful shimmer to your pieces. The material is so versatile that it can replicate many other objects from nature, as well as man-made materials.

Straight from the package, polymer clay is firm and requires a little kneading to make it pliable enough to shape (called "conditioning"). The length of time it takes to condition your clay will depend on the brand you choose. The more widely available clays, from softest to firmest (before conditioning), are Sculpey III as the softest, then Premo! Sculpey, Kato Polyclay, Fimo Soft and then Fimo Classic. Although this is a consideration when choosing a clay brand, I believe that the tensile strength (flexibility after curing) is also very important, especially when creating jewelry that will be handled a lot. Personally I use Premo! Sculpey, as it is easy to knead and is quite strong and flexible after baking. It is also readily available in a large selection of colors. Other brands of clay that may be available in your area are Cernit, Formello and Modello. You may mix any of the different clay brand colors together.

All polymer clay brands share this feature: The warmer it gets, the softer it gets. These clays will not air-dry, so they can be left out while working and will not dry out. They only become permanently hard after they are cured (baked) in an oven at a specific temperature. It is a fabulous medium to use with various surface techniques, as you will see in this book. It may seem like my studio consists of white clay only as you begin to browse through the book projects, but be assured, I use all of the wonderful colors available. I just wanted this book to emphasize combining various mediums with the clay that are open to further exploration. I do, however, purchase and use at least four times the amount of white clay, compared to any other color.

CLAY COLORS

You can purchase colors and mix them together in any color you can imagine. These are color-mixed swatches

CONDITIONING

Immediately after removing polymer clay from the outer wrapper, it will be too firm to work with. The clay must be conditioned to make it soft and pliable. This is an important step that should not be skipped.

If you're using one of the firmer clays, cut a section of the cube into small slices (like slicing bread) with a paring knife or stiff slicing blade. Warm the clay pieces by placing them in your hand and making a fist. The warmth of your hand will cause the clay to become soft enough to pass through a hand-crank pasta machine. You may benefit from using a clay-dedicated food processor on the "pulse" setting to break up extra-firm clay into tiny pieces before rolling it. You can also add a clay softener to clay that is too firm.

A good way to calculate how much conditioning the clay will require, either by kneading or passing through the pasta machine, is to mix two colors of clay together. Once the clay becomes a new solid hue, it is ready and workable.

A good way to judge if clay is well-conditioned is to bend the sheet in half. If cracking occurs at the bend, it's not ready. Continue conditioning until you achieve a smooth, seamless fold.

STORAGE

Polymer clay begins to harden once it reaches 90°F (32°C), it's important to store it indoors in a cool (but not cold) place. *Don't* leave it in your car on a sunny day or in direct sunlight near a window. Also, don't store it in a cold garage as it will stiffen up and be harder to work with. Although the clay does not air-dry, it's good to store it in plastic bags to keep it clean from dust, pet hair and similar contaminates. Be aware also that some plastic containers are not suitable for raw, uncured clay. Over time, the clay will actually begin to melt into the plastic-making it sticky and unusable. Always test plastic containers before placing unbaked clay in them.

SIZING CLAY

At times my instructions will direct you to form a certain-size ball to begin with and then shape it or roll it flat. In this case use the chart above. For example, I have called a ⅜-inch (10mm) size ball an "extra-small ball," a ⅝-inch (16mm) ball a "small ball," a ⅞-inch (22mm) ball a "medium-sized ball" and so on. These are just my estimates on how much clay you will need to form a shape. Do not confuse these sizes with specific sizes listed for a project.

You can use a plastic circle template with measurements marked on it to accurately gauge different specific-sized balls of clay. Roll the ball to the approximate size first. If it just fits snugly through a hole in the template, it will be that size. Refer to the template photo on page 75 in step 1 of the *Sicilian Spice Bracelet* project.

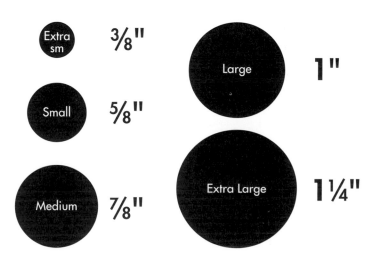

CLAY BALL SIZES

Extra sm — ⅜"

Small — ⅝"

Medium — ⅞"

Large — 1"

Extra Large — 1¼"

POLYMER CLAY TOOLS

Besides your hands, there are many items that make great tools for working the clay. Some are created specifically for polymer clay, some are common things you probably have in your own kitchen or toolbox. In this section of the book I have grouped the photos into categories, which have similar uses. The great thing about these tools, are that most of them have multiple functions. The tools are numbered so you can easily identify them in the photos and the corresponding text.

WORK SURFACES

A Formica, acrylic, Plexiglas, glass or marble work surface is best. When making jewelry, I often work directly on a smooth, ceramic baking tile to avoid having to move the piece before baking. The tile surface is also excellent for polymer clay as it allows it to stick when you need it to, and the clay is easily removed with a non-serrated flexible kitchen knife or slicing blade. Do not work directly on fine furniture, as the clay can damage the finish.

FLATTENING TOOLS

The Makin's Professional Ultimate Clay Machine (1) is similar to a hand-crank pasta machine, although this one is created specifically for polymer clay with 7-inch (18cm) long, non-stick rollers and 9 different thickness settings. There are other brands of pasta machines available with 6-inch (15cm) long metal rollers, with 7 settings, which can be substituted. These are used to create smooth, even sheets of clay and are a necessary tool to form graduated color blends. Besides my hands, my pasta machine is my most frequently used tool. Its ability to evenly flatten and 'stretch' the clay in a sense makes it invaluable. I also use it to initially conditioning the clay, making this task much easier and faster. This conditioning process can be sped up, by attaching a Makin's Professional Ultimate Clay Machine Motor, which replaces the handle. This motor is useful as it helps prevent strain on your hand and arm muscles.

When flattening the clay in the pasta machine, always begin with the thickest setting, and work your way through each consecutive setting until you reach the desired thickness. In other words, if your thickest setting is no. 1, and a project calls for a sheet that is rolled at the fourth thickest setting, run the sheet though at no. 1, no. 2, no. 3 and then no. 4. I have removed the front and back plates from my pasta machine, as they really are not necessary. Please note that some pasta machines are manufactured with the highest number as the thickest setting.

Instead of a pasta machine, you can also use an acrylic rolling rod (2) to flatten the clay. Even with my pasta machine, I use a roller to take out imperfections or to start a flattening process slowly, such as when I am "stretching" chalk pods onto a clay base.

A clay-dedicated food processor can also be useful in breaking up extra-firm pieces of clay before rolling (not pictured).

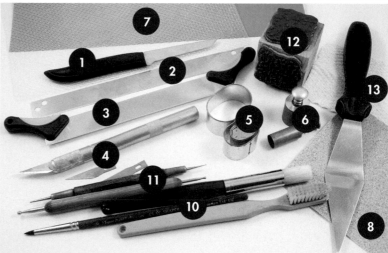

CUTTING TOOLS

Using the correct cutting tool will make a job much easier and successful. A non-serrated kitchen paring knife (1) makes cutting clay pieces off of a new cube of clay an easy task. I use a long, rigid slicing blade (2) when I need to make straight cuts on a clay sheet, or when cutting clay into slices before conditioning.

When my design requires a slight curve, I pick up a long, thin cutting blade, also called a clay slicer (3), as I can flex the blade while cutting. These thin blades are also essential for cutting very thin slices of millefiori cane work.

For detail work such as cutting precise shapes, a craft blade knife (4) works well. This tool has detachable blades that can be changed out when they become dull. Simply rotate the textured area of the metal housing to loosen its grip on the blade (which is very sharp!). There are many blade attachments for craft blade knives, but I only keep the standard no. 11 blades on hand.

There are small cutter shapes available in almost every design imaginable. I have used this particular oval cutter set (5) by Makin's Clay in this book. I also get a lot of use out of my mini Kemper Pattern Cutters (6).

Texturing tools can be something as simple as a piece of cloth (7) or sand paper (8). I often use a stiff, flat-ended stencil brush (9) or even an old toothbrush (10) for a subtle texture that also takes away the clay's natural shine when a matte finish is desired. Various sized double-ended stylus tools (11) are handy for creating dots. Rubber tipped versions can aid in smoothing clay seams.

Rubber stamps (12) are available with texture designs as well as Scratch Art's Shade-Tex Rubbing Plates (13) which are flexible plastic and come in a large variety of designs.

TEXTURING TOOLS

There's a huge variety of rubber stamps (1) just waiting to be use on polymer or metal clay. Choose deeply etched designs. Rollagraph Stamp Wheels (2) are another great source for designs that can be applied continuously.

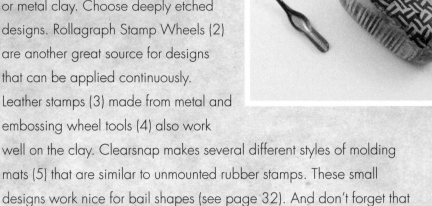

Leather stamps (3) made from metal and embossing wheel tools (4) also work well on the clay. Clearsnap makes several different styles of molding mats (5) that are similar to unmounted rubber stamps. These small designs work nice for bail shapes (see page 32). And don't forget that you can use found objects such as bobby pins (6), textured leaves (7) or even paper clips (8) for some interesting impression tools.

FINE LINE CARVING TOOL

To create your own carving tool, form an extra-large ball of well-conditioned scrap clay into a fat log shape. Decorate the surface as desired. Apply a few drops of quick-dry cyanoacrylate glue to the base of the blade and press the base into the clay. Bake the tool for the full length recommended for this very thick amount of clay and allow the clay to cool.

MIXED MEDIA MATERIALS

It's so rewarding to set aside time to "play" with polymer clay with the goal of combining it with completely different mediums. Listed here are only a few options. It's my hope that this list will inspirer you to do some of your own mixed media experiments.

I often use glossy powders or Tim Holtz Distress Embossing Powders (1) for a gritty texture. Embossing powders are activated when heated, so they come to life after baking. Mica powders, (2) such as Pearl Ex Pigment Powders, are extra fine powders that can be brushed onto the clay surface for a lovely colored metallic appearance. Artists' soft pastel chalks (3) are one of my favorite materials. I like to purchase chalk sets with half-size sticks. I get twice as many colors, and the half size is more than enough. Keep wet wipes nearby when you work, to clean chalk from your fingers. Piñata alcohol inks (4) are used to tint liquid clay and are available in many bright, fun colors.

Krylon silver and gold leafing pens (5) are great for outlining baked clay as well as giving the back of your pieces a finished look. Another form of metallic accents are very thin sheets of silver and gold leaf (6). The leaf sticks to unbaked clay, or it can be applied to baked clay pieces using leafing adhesive (7).

To add images to the clay surface, I have had success using Avery brand iron-on inkjet t-shirt transfer paper, specifically for white or light fabrics. Copyright-free image books by Dover are a great source for artwork for your jewelry. I also enjoy adding wire (8) to my work. It's available in different thicknesses of metallic colors, and the FunWire brand has vinyl-coated opaque-colored wires that actually bond to the clay when baked.

To add a contrast I like to incorporate pre-made wool felt beads (9) that have loose, colorful wool roving (10) needle felted to the surface. Soft elements such as fancy fibers and cording (11) gives polymer clay pieces a soft, feminine style. And for a final elegant touch, I like to add various sizes and styles of glass beads (12) and crystal beads (13) (Swarovski is a favorite). These extra touches can turn a good piece into a great one, adding sparkle and value to clay jewelry.

MISCELLANEOUS TOOLS

At times you will need to poke holes into the clay or through beads. I use a double-ended needle tool (1) to make small holes and a knitting needle (2) for large holes. The paddle end of the needle tool (3) can be used to scrape excess clay grout from mini mosaics. Another tool used for making holes in beads are small drill bits (4). These come in handy to enlarge holes in cured beads when the pins or cord don't quite fit inside.

I use four basic types of glues throughout the book, which have various uses, All-purpose E6000 or Goop glue from Eclectic (5), quick-dry cyanoacrylate gel glue (6), two-part epoxy glue (7) and G-S Hypo Cement (8).

A clear ruler (9) and a flexible sewing tape measure (10) are also used throughout the book. Flat paintbrushes (11) are handy for applying wet mediums to the clay, although for fine powders I like to use a large, very soft round brush (12). Various grits of wet dry sandpaper (13) are used to sand the clay's surface.

RELEASE AGENTS

There are two basic types of release agents, wet or dry. Either of these will prevent the clay from sticking to other objects such as molds or rubber stamps. Plain water, sprayed from a extra fine mist spray bottle, can be used as a good all-around release agent. You can also use cornstarch or baby powder (14) if a dry release is desired. The only drawback is that occasionally powders can remain on the clay after baking. Not to worry, though, as this residue can be rinsed clean with water once the clay has cooled.

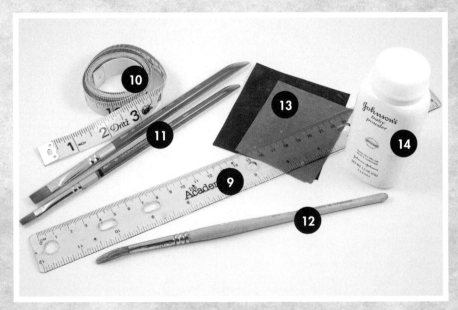

CLAY SCRAPS

The great thing about polymer clay is that there is never any waste. Once you've been working (or should I say "playing?") with the clay, you will undoubtedly have some clay bits and pieces left over.

I won't even try to list *all* the ways to use scrap clay, but let me share just a few ideas to get you started. A common use for scrap clay is to use it to form bead bases. I also use a lot of my scraps to make clay molds. Scrap clay can even be used to create a double-ended clay tool, which is ideal for placing stones into clay.

You can also keep a soft lump of clay (translucent clay works well) close to your pasta machine and run it through the rollers often to clean any loose clay particles. And scraps can be lumped together and passed through a clay extruder, resulting in a similar look to a bull's-eye cane.

You can lessen the amount of distortion of millefiori cane ends with scrap clay (see "Felt Bead Neckpiece" on page 110). Before reducing your cane, form scrap clay into a log that is the same diameter as your current cane. Cut the log in half, making each of these "extensions" about half the length of the original cane. Firmly press the logs onto the ends of your cane, smooth the seam and then reduce the cane as usual.

Another way to use scraps or clay colors that didn't come out as you desired is to brush mica powders over the clay or add a metallic leafing sheet. So save those scraps!

ART FROM SCRAPS

This unique pin is a great example of what you can do with scrap clay. The artist put together scraps with a nice color scheme and then rolled them through her pasta machine. She added digital art using a liquid polymer clay transferring technique and framed her piece with a clay bezel, which is formed around metal cutter shapes and baked. Instant art!

Scrap B
Pam Sanders
Photo by the artist

DOUBLE-ENDED POINTED CLAY TOOL

Create your own double-ended pointed clay tool for positioning and pressing stones into clay. Using a pencil sharpener or 220-grit sandpaper, sharpen both ends of a wooden dowel to a dull point. Shape two clay balls into pointed cone shapes. Press *one* over a dowel end. Bake as directed and cool down. (Wood is safe in an oven at this low temperature.) Press the remaining clay cone over the other end of the tool. Do *not* bake this; this is the raw clay end you will use to pick up and position flat-back stones.

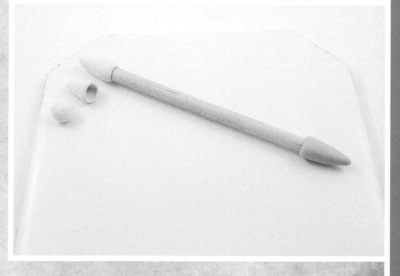

CURING

Polymer clay will not air dry. It must be baked in an oven, toaster oven or convection oven to become permanently hard.

I place my pieces on smooth ceramic baking tiles. If I am making a double-sided piece or beads, I place them on an index card or piece of cardstock first and then onto my ceramic baking tile. This prevents flat, shiny spots from forming on the clay.

SAFETY TIP

Always use a timer when baking your clay. If it does burn, remove it from the oven with a potholder and place it outside. Do not breathe the fumes.

CURING TOOLS

I use a Clay & Craft Oven (1) by AMACO, created specifically for baking polymer clay. It turns off automatically when the built-in timer goes off, which is a real plus to prevent scorching or burning the clay.

Baking times and temperatures will vary between the different brands, so follow the instructions on the package to fully cure your projects. The length of time you bake a piece will be determined by how thick the clay is. It is best to use a separate oven thermometer (2), placed on the rack of your oven to gauge the temperature accuracy. A handheld heat gun (3) is also a useful tool to heat-set liquid clay and layers of floor finish used as a glaze on the clay.

FINISHING

There are several ways to finish polymer clay jewelry. Baked clay can be left as is, with no finish at all, if desired. The projects in this book will suggest a particular finish the choice is really up to you. In some cases you may wish to sand and buff a piece. Use gray or black wet/dry sandpaper for sanding. Place a drop of liquid dish soap (1) into a sink or tub of water. Start out with a lower grit such as 400, and gradually work your way up to a higher grit, dipping your clay piece and the sandpaper in water often. Clean away the clay residue with an old, toothbrush.

After sanding you will want to buff your clay piece with denim (2) or T-shirt fabric or with an electric buffing wheel (3). Use an unstitched muslin wheel on the buffer, as felt and other types of wheels will gouge your clay. You can find many resources online with instructions on buffing if you decide on this finish. Always wear protective eyewear and follow instructions carefully or your piece will go shooting through the air and damage whatever is in its path.

I usually use floor finish (4) to give my pieces a gloss finish. I apply a coat while the piece is still very warm from the oven and then heat the clay with a handheld heat gun to dry it. I repeat adding another coat while the piece is still very warm from the heat gun to apply two or more additional coats. I allow the final coat to air-dry.

If you want your piece to shine like glass, the highest gloss finish I have found is a two-part high gloss resin coating (such as Enviro-Tex-Lite) (5). It is very thick and will give the surface of your piece tremendous depth. One coat of resin is equivalent to several applications of other glazes. The drawbacks are that it has a strong odor, and, if it's allowed to migrate over the sides of the clay, it forms drips that need to be cleaned away periodically throughout the drying time. If you want the ultimate glossy finish, though, the work is worth it.

Make sure whichever glaze you select is polymer-clay friendly. Some sprays and brush-on liquid glazes will have a chemical reaction to the clay. These finishes will never completely cure, and after several days your clay will become sticky. Always test a glaze, watching it for a few weeks if you can, before you use it on your work.

SAFETY TIP

Always wear safety eyewear and pull back long hair or lose clothing when using an electric buffing wheel. Position your clay piece on the bottom third area of the buffing wheel at all times. This way, if a clay piece breaks away, it will travel under the wheel and shoot off away from you. Don't use an electric buffing wheel around children, pets or glass windows. I also recommend placing a large fabric-lined box behind the buffing wheel to catch any flying clay pieces.

SAFETY TIP

Use only wet/dry sandpaper under running water or in a tub of water when sanding polymer clay, as you do not want to breathe in the clay dust.

MIXING CLAY COLORS

Color is what first attracted me to polymer clay. I have always loved color, and the fact that I could mix any color imaginable was a real plus for my custom jewelry. Mixing clay colors is similar to mixing paint, although much easier to measure. Specific amounts can be cut directly from a clay cube, punched out of a flattened clay sheet with cutters or rolled into same-size clay balls. Using these methods will make creating custom hues easier to duplicate for future projects. Colors tend to deepen when baked, so mix a little white clay into your custom colors to keep them bright.

It's a good idea to document how many parts of each color you have used for a new hue. Also, bake a swatch of all your color mixes for reference, so you will have actual baked samples and a color recipe to follow in the future. I label my color swatches before baking them by etching numbers onto them with a tiny ball stylus tool. I also write down and then type the recipe (number of parts used of each packaged color) that corresponds to the color number. Taking a few minutes to document your formulas will save you time and money in the future!

I've enjoyed mixing colors so much that years ago I self-published a "Fimo Color Mixing Chart." A large miniatures company bought the entire batch of printed leaflets and distributed them to craft stores across the country. I share this with you as a preface to explain that my knowledge of color and color mixing is much broader today. It's still exciting to create new color mixes the old-fashioned way, but as we progress and discover our personal color palette preferences, there is an advantage to finding new ways to create and duplicate these colors.

BLENDING COLORS

There are a variety of ways to measure portions of clay to create new colors. The amount of a new color needed for a project will determine which technique is appropriate. I have included the following three color methods for you to try. You may come up with your own system that works well for you. Experiment and have fun mixing new colors!

THE COLOR OF POLYMER CLAY

Polymer clay can produce spectacular color. Here, the vibrant hues combine with the subtle lines and shading (created with a millefiori technique) produce a striking piece. These flat-back beads, reminiscent of strokes of oil paint, make the design come to life.

Green Blue Petal Bracelet
Sarah Shriver
Photo by George Post

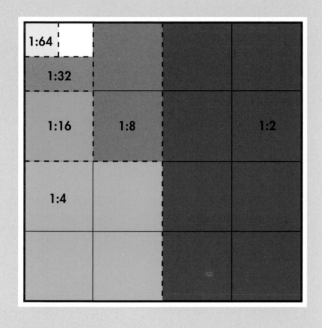

Cutting Portions from the Cube

For larger quantities of color mixes you can score and cut sections directly off of the clay cubes and then condition them while you are mixing the pieces together to save a step. Using this ratio diagram as a measurement guide, cut as many parts off of each cube color as called for in the recipe. Smaller amounts of new colors can also be measured by rolling sheets of conditioned clay, then using the diagram to cut the amounts required.

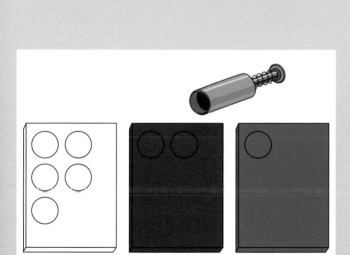

Using Small Cutter Shapes

If you only need a small amount of a color, you can roll sheets of conditioned clay through the pasta machine's thickest setting and cut out shapes with a Kemper pattern cutter. Each shape would represent one part. This technique is especially useful for color recipes that have uneven parts. This diagram illustrates the recipe: 5 parts white + 2 parts red + 1 part blue. Punch out circles, then mix them together thoroughly.

The "Skinner Blend"

There have been extreme advances and new techniques in mixing color since I first began playing with polymer clay. The "Skinner Blend" method, discovered and graciously shared by Judith Skinner, allows us to create graduated color blended sheets using a pasta machine. The colors graduate seamlessly into the next. This technique has taken my artwork to a new level and it can do the same for yours.

1 Roll each preconditioned clay color through the thickest pasta machine setting. Fold the clay from one corner to the opposite corner.

2 Secure the folded triangle edges together, placing them slightly offset to each other. Trim the extended triangle shape of each color so the clay forms a rectangle or square.

3 Roll the clay sheet through the thickest pasta machine setting, with both colors touching the rollers. Fold the clay sheet in half onto itself so the two edges of the same color meet. (In other words, bring the bottom edge up to the top edge.) Press the clay together. Run the sheet through the pasta machine once again, with the fold against the rollers, at the thickest setting.

4 Repeat folding and rolling the clay through the pasta machine, making sure both colors touch the rollers each time. You will see the colors begin to marbleize. This photo shows the sheet after 10 cycles through the machine.

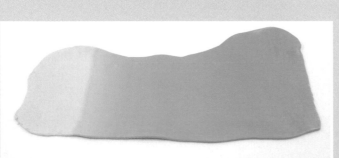

5 Repeat folding and running the clay through the pasta machine until the colors blend seamlessly. This usually takes approximately 25 to 35 times. If you still see color streaks in the clay sheet, the blend is not yet complete. Continue folding and rolling.

LIQUID CLAY IN APPLICATOR BOTTLE

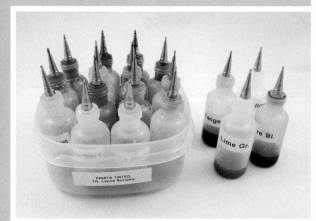

PRE-MIXING COLORS

Since I use a lot of liquid polymer clay, I have a whole collection of pre-tinted clay in applicator bottles. This saves me time, because I don't have to stop working to mix more colors. There's no need to place an additional lid on the metal tips, but if you'd like to close up the hole, you can slide an eye pin into the tip. I store my applicator bottles in inexpensive plastic containers.

TINTING LIQUID POLYMER CLAY

To color liquid polymer clay, I use a small six-welled palette. I determine my range of colors, then (working on a protected surface) I fill as many wells as I need with liquid polymer clay. I add one small drop of alcohol ink or a pinch of powdered pigment to each well, then stir with the stylus to add color to the liquid.

WORKING WITH LIQUID POLYMER CLAY

Liquid polymer clay is an exciting form of polymer clay that has taken the clay world by storm. There are a variety of liquid polymer clays available from different manufacturers, with slightly different characteristics. Some liquid clays are thinner, some are shiny after bake or have a matte finish. I've experimented most with Translucent Liquid Sculpey (TLS), and prefer it for jewelry making. It has many uses. It is the thickest brand, and can be hardened with a heat gun before it has a chance to spread out and flatten; this makes it great for achieving certain textures. It can be used as glue that sets as it bakes, or as a top coat to protect the surface. It can be mixed with alcohol inks, oil paints, powdered pigments such as mica powders or artist chalk pastels. There are too many techniques to list, but you can explore this medium by checking out Ann and Karen Mitchell's ground-breaking book entitled, you guessed it, *Liquid Polymer Clay* by Krause Publications.

You can apply liquid polymer clay in a variety of ways. It can be squeezed directly from a bottle tip, or you can apply it with a brush or stylus. Or, to get a fine line application, I fill a small Jacquard's plastic applicator bottle with liquid clay and replace the lid and plastic tip with an extra-fine metal tip.

The applicator bottle works well with larger cells, but filling smaller cells is often only possible with a stylus.

WORKING WITH METAL CLAY

Adding fine silver accents will not only add interest to a design, but will increase the value of your work substantially. If you haven't tried working with the new metal clays, the projects in this book are a good starting point.

Metal clay is made up of microscopic particles of real silver, suspended in a binder. The clay can be shaped, textured, cut and manipulated just like other clays. Once it dries, it needs to be fired so the binder can burn off, resulting in a piece of fine silver that is .999 pure. (Sterling silver is .925.) Silver metal clay will become white after firing. This is not a coating. What you see are actually tiny particles standing on end. Brushing and burnishing the metal clay will flatten them, causing the surface to reflect silver. Further polishing or buffing will cause the shine to become even brighter.

Metal clay, unlike polymer clay, can air-dry. So, when working with metal clay, the best advice I can give is to plan ahead. Gather all of the supplies you will need, including basic supplies and those listed in project instructions. Avoid touching the clay too much, as your hands will dry it out; for example, use plastic wrap on the surface when rolling the clay flat. If the clay becomes dry, spritz it with a little water. Keep olive oil handy for your fingers and tools. Always put extra pieces of metal clay back into the original airtight container as soon as you can to keep it fresh and moist.

Metal clay comes in a variety of sizes and forms. The projects in this book use lump form, which is similar to traditional clays. It comes in an airtight pouch that will keep it moist and pliable. The pad or ball of clay in the package will seem like a small amount, until you begin working with it. You'll see that a little goes a long way.

I use PMC3, which is low-fire metal clay, meaning it can be fired with a small handheld butane torch (the same type used for crème brûlée). The advantage is that you can try the clay without purchasing an expensive kiln.

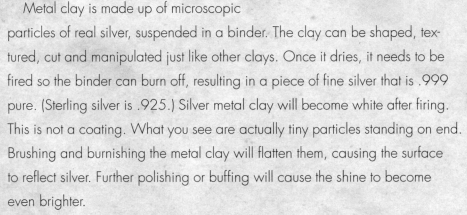

EVENING THE ODDS

In this book, the first step in all of the metal clay projects is to create a clay slab with a uniform thickness using an acrylic roller and playing cards stacked on either side (the number of cards will vary with the project). Rub olive oil on the roller to prevent it from sticking to the metal clay.

SAFETY ISSUES

- Make sure to allow your metal clay to dry completely before firing it.

- Use extreme caution when using a butane torch. It is important to pay attention to what you are doing, the entire firing cycle. Try not to get distracted.

- Always wear safety eyewear and pull back long hair when torch-firing.

- Place your clay piece on a firing block that is placed on heat-proof surface. This way, if your piece happens to get away from you, it will not harm your counter or table.

METAL CLAY TOOLS

Here is a basic tool list for working with metal clay. Some of these items you may have around the house already, especially if you already work with polymer clay. You will use a brass buff burnishing brush (1) and a steel spoon (2) to burnish your clay; an extra-fine mist spray bottle (3) to keep your metal clay moist while working; olive oil as a release agent; a small handheld butane torch (4) and refill cans of butane (5). You will also use a small acrylic roller and small stack of playing cards (6); variously sized plastic straws (7); a nonstick craft sheet (Ranger) (8); a firing block for torch-firing (9); a filing stick/emery board (10) and fine-grain sandpaper (11); a craft blade knife; long fibergrip tweezers (12); a small liner paintbrush (13); sheets of wet/dry polishing papers (14); small Kemper pattern cutters; and a tapered candle for making rings.

There are some specialty tools you may find yourself using. These include Makin's Professional Ultimate Clay Extruder Stainless Steel Edition for metal clay and adaptor disks (15), liver of sulfur (16); coffee cup warmer or electric warming plate (17); non-stick balm or similar release agent (18); steel mesh (19); a metal file (20); and hand conditioner to keep clay from sticking to your hands (21).

Metal Clay Processes

The metal clay used throughout this book has a few unique procedures that diverge from polymer clay's. Metal clay should be completely dry, for example, before firing. You can speed the drying process by placing them on a coffee cup warmer, an electric warming plate or in a food dehydrator, if you have one. When your pieces are dry, they are still very fragile, so handle carefully. This is the stage when pieces can break. With a light touch, sand any rough edges now, before firing, using an emery board. Fine grit sand paper may also be used. After sanding, you're ready to torch-fire and then burnish your piece.

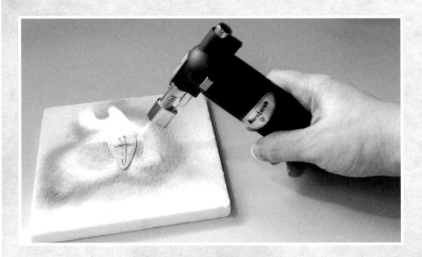

1 Torch-fire the dried metal clay

Place your piece on a firing block or soldering block. Make sure the torch is filled with butane fuel. Ignite the torch and hold it about 1½" (4cm) from the metal clay. Move the torch constantly over the metal clay while firing. In just a short time, a flame and a little smoke will appear, which means the binder is burning off.

2 Watch for a pink-orange color

Soon you will notice the metal clay piece begin to turn pink with orange edges. This is normal and will bring you closer to the full heat stage.

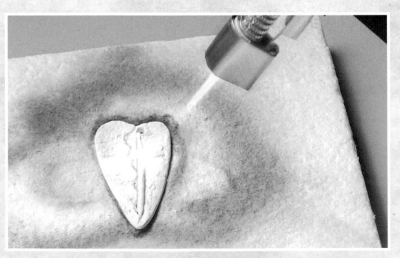

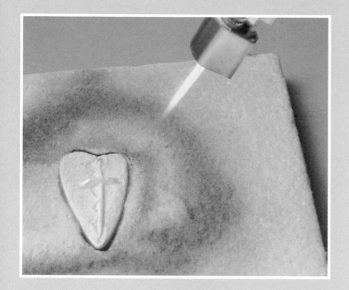

3 Hold the piece at the red stage

When your piece begins to glow a red-orange color, hold this color for a full 2 minutes, or a little longer if your piece is large. If at any point you see silver areas, pull the torch away from the piece as it is starting to melt, and continue to keep the red glow.

4 Cool the piece

Do not touch the metal clay! Allow it to cool, or quench it in ice-cold water using fiber-grip tweezers to pick it up.

5 Burnish the Piece

Using a brass buff burnishing brush, brush both sides of the metal clay surfaces to cause the particles to reflect a satin silver sheen.

6 Bring up the shine

You may leave your metal clay as is, or you may bring up the shine by burnishing further using a metal object such as the paddle end of a needle tool (shown), a smooth spoon handle or a metal clay burnishing tool. I often shine only part of a piece for contrast. To achieve a mirror finish as seen on the cross, you may buff portions of your piece, for contrast, or the entire surface, with polishing papers.

BASIC JEWELRY ASSEMBLY

There is no one, single way to assemble your jewelry pieces. You can add a simple closure, or make one so elaborate it become integral part of the piece.

Whatever you choose to do, there are a few jewelry assembly tools I recommend. Two types of pliers are used to create or bend items in this book: needle nose and round nose. You'll also need eye pins, pin backs, head pins and buna cord or other necklace cords.

Jump rings are essential, and a jump ring tool is a great alternative to holding open a jump ring with multiple pairs of pliers.

BAILS

A metal clay bail can add quit a bit to the final piece. The top bail (by the author) was textured by pressing chopped-up metal clay scraps onto an oval shape that was folded over a straw. The bottom center bail (by Melanie Dilday) was created by wrapping a long, thin triangle of metal clay around a birthday cake candle, overlapping the tip of the triangle around the base. The silver of the tube bails (also by artist Melanie Dilday) provides a wonderful contrast to the color and texture of the fiber necklaces (right and left).

END CAPS & CLOSURES

There are many ways to finish necklaces. One of my personal favorites when making a clay piece is to continue the theme and design by creating matching end caps. You can mimic cone ends as Melanie Dilday did (bottom and left) to finish off her twisted fiber cords. And Tina Holden created the clever ends with starfish-covered brass ends (right). At times I like to keep the closure simple, but also complement a pendant or bead necklace. For this I add a clay bead to the end of a buna cord and finish the opposite end with a loop that's glued into a clay tube bead (top).

Pin Backs

1 Add four tiny drops of quick-dry cyanoacrylate glue to the back side of the pin bar and press in place. Allow the glue to dry.

2 Form a clay strip by rolling an extra-small ball of the same clay color and flatten to approximately 1/32" (1mm) thick. Stamp your signature or the date as desired and cut into a strip just long enough to cover the bar of the pin. Add four tiny drops of quick-dry glue to the bar.

3 To secure the clay strip, press it in place over the pin back bar and smooth the edges. Place the project on a blank index card or piece of cardstock and re-bake for 15 minutes, at the recommended temperature of your clay brand.

Beaded Eye Pins

1 Thread the bead(s) onto the eye pin. Clip the pin with wire cutters or the wire cutting area of needle-nose pliers, leaving a 3/8" (10mm) straight area beyond the last bead. Notice which direction the original eye pin loop is facing and form the second loop to match. Bend the pin to a 90° angle as close to the last bead as possible. Do not force the pliers into the beads as they may chip or break.

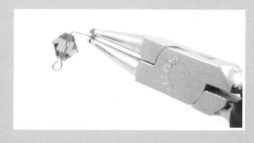

2 Measure and mark a reference line 1/18" (1mm) from the tip of your round-nose pliers, using a permanent felt-tip pen. Grasp the end of the pin with the pliers, positioning the pin at the marking.

3 Rotate the pliers to form a loop in the pin, leaving it slightly open to attach to your project. Slightly open the opposite eye pin loop with needle-nose pliers, to form a hook, so it is ready to be inserted into a project ring or loop. Once secure, close the loop with needle-nose pliers.

These instructions can also be used to create a loop at the end of a head pin.

Fabricated Bails

Using a metal clay bail can add a professional and finished look to your jewelry. Creating metal clay bails is a simple process. Texture can be added to the clay using rubber stamps, texture sheets and rubbing plates. The designs can be accentuated after firing using a solution of liver of sulfur, dissolved in warm water, to add a patina to the bails. Shapes can easily be cut from a flattened sheet of metal clay with small clay and pattern cutters. To create a nice permanent curve in the bails, you can place the pieces over plastic drinking straws as they dry.

MATERIALS

Basic metal clay materials and tools

25gm silver PMC3 (metal clay)

Two sizes of plastic drinking straws

Various textures (rubber stamps, texture sheets, etc.)

Liver of sulfur (optional patina solution)

NOTE

I have listed a little more metal clay under "materials" than you might need for the project. I feel it is better to have a little extra, than not enough.

1 Make the test bails

I'm not used to clay drying out as I work, so I always create test bails with non-metal polymer clay before I even open my metal clay package. To do this, roll some scrap polymer clay on the second thickest pasta machine setting. Experiment by adding different textures and cut out various bail shapes. (The metal embossing tool pictured has a large herringbone pattern). Drape the bail shapes over drinking straws and see how they perform. There is no need to bake these samples unless you'd like to keep them for reference. As you can't bake the straws, replace them with rolled-up pieces of foil.

2 Create a negative mold

If you'd like your metal clay to duplicate the raised rubber stamp design, you must first make an "innie" mold. Run a sheet of scrap clay through the thickest pasta machine setting. Mist the area of the rubber or stamp with water and press clay onto the design. Remove the clay, allow the mold to dry and bake for the recommended time.

3 Add texture and cut the bails

Place a stack of 3 playing cards on each side of a nonstick craft sheet. Rub a thin layer of oil on the rolling rod, place the metal clay on the sheet and roll with the rolling rod to flatten. The thickness will become equal with the height of the cards. Brush oil onto the texturing tool (whether that be a stamp, rubbing plate, polymer clay mold or metal embossing tool) and use it to apply the texture design to the clay. Lift the metal clay and place it on a nonstick craft sheet. Cut out the final bail shape with a craft blade knife.

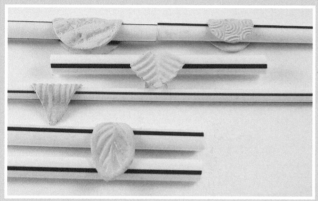

4 Shape the bails

Drape the bails over a small or regular-sized drinking straw, depending on the space required for your cording and the clay piece. If your polymer clay piece will be thick, use two straws side by side as seen in the leaf bail (bottom center). Allow them to dry until they are leather-hard and then carefully slide them off of the straw. Let them completely dry. The pieces are still very fragile at this point, so handle them carefully. Lightly sand any rough edges with 600-grit sandpaper.

5 Fire, burnish and buff the bails

Torch-fire the bails individually, then burnish. You may add a patina if desired to darken the impression of the texture by using a liver of sulfur solution after the piece is burnished. Follow the directions on the liver of sulfur container to dissolve one chunk. Have a separate glass of cold water close by to stop the patina process when you're satisfied with the result. I use a large paper clip to hold my pieces while dipping them. Buff the bails with buffing paper (bottom right) to bring up the shine on the raised areas.

6 Secure the bails

Here are four finished samples. The top left bail has been burnished and dipped for a short time into the sulfur patina. At the top right is the text bail. It was dipped for a longer time in the patina until it became brown. The bottom left bail was just burnished and buffed with buffing paper and the bottom right bail was dipped the longest in the sulfur and then buffed slightly. Secure the bails to your clay pendants using a two-part epoxy adhesive.

NOTE

Most of the bail samples in these instructions have been added to various pendants throughout the book.

SECTION TWO

Projects

Although each project in this section uses one or more techniques and mediums, the jewelry pieces are grouped together by one prominent material that has been added. You'll find projects with artists' soft pastel chalks, heat-activated transfer techniques, silver and gold leaf, embossing powders, techniques for tinting liquid polymer clay, metal clay additions, mini-mosaic projects and even felting techniques and fun fibers for a soft but spectacular finale!

Altered Pastel Brooch

Our first project uses the chalk-scraping technique, which is a good starting point. I could have easily named this project "Sprinkle, Smear and Twist," as that is what you'll be doing to alter the pattern for this fun surface treatment. If you are not new to polymer clay, pull out your scraps, as we'll be making a clay mold first. If you are a newbie, you can use new clay for this step until you build up your own collection of scraps, and trust me, you will!

MATERIALS

White, frost (bleached translucent) and scrap polymer clay

Translucent Liquid Sculpey clay

Cornstarch or baby powder

Soft pastel chalk set

Textured watercolor paper or cardstock for a palette

5mm Swarovski aquamarine point back crystal stone

G-S Hypo Cement

Quick-dry cyanoacrylate glue

Wet wipes

Extra-fine beading needle

Future floor finish

1½" (4cm) long bar pin back

Acrylic roller

Grease pencil

Wet/dry sandpaper

Craft blade knife

Slicing blade

Extra-fine mist spray bottle

Linoleum cutter

Polymer clay softener

Soft cloth

Pasta machine

TIP

When you are using brand new pastel chalks, rub the flat surfaces of the sticks with a cotton swab to slightly rough them up. You will be able to achieve a more saturated color application.

1 Sculpt the original shape

Using a ball of well-conditioned scrap clay, form a domed, cabochon-style shape. I formed a flat back football shape and then curved the tips in opposite directions. Bake the clay as directed for this very thick piece. When the clay is completely cool, wet-sand the surface until very smooth. Form a similar shaped thick pad of scrap clay to use as the mold. Dust the original shape and all sides of the (blue) mold clay thoroughly with cornstarch or baby powder.

2 Make and bake the mold

Press the original shape into the mold clay until the bottom side of the original shape is even with the mold. Gently move the sides of the mold away from the original and remove the shape. If the original is difficult to remove, you may either place it in the freezer for 5 minutes before de-molding, or you can use a "scrap handle" (shown in step 6). Bake the mold as directed and allow it to cool completely.

3 Sprinkle and smear the chalks

Roll a sheet of white clay to 1/16" (2mm) thick (third thickest pasta setting) and place on cardstock. Rub the side edge of a fuchsia pastel chalk stick over paper. Using your finger, apply this chalk in a circle motion to cover the clay surface. Hold a deep blue pastel chalk stick above the clay and scrape particles onto random areas with your fingernail or a craft blade knife. Add particles of bright blue and fuchsia. Using your finger, smear the chalk particles in a curved line, leaving a small fuchsia space between rows. Scrape particles of pink over the darkest areas. Press the clay with the acrylic roller to secure the chalk particles.

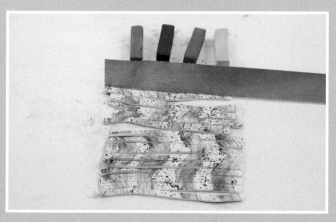

4 Decorate the back side and cut into strips

Flip the sheet over to the back side. Leave the background of this side of the clay white for contrast. Scrap particles of bright blue, deep green and royal blue chalk and smear into curved rows as in the previous step. Scrap particles of aqua chalk over the darkest color areas. Roll over the clay once using the roller to secure the chalk particles. Using a stiff slicing blade, cut the sheet of clay into 1/8" (3mm) wide horizontal strips.

5 Twist and secure the strips

Lift one clay strip, hold it at both ends and loosely twist it in opposite directions so both color sides are showing. Secure the strips side by side to cover the white slab. Roll over the clay once with an acrylic roller, and then flatten through the pasta machine at the no. 2, no. 3 and no. 4 settings.

6 Mold the base

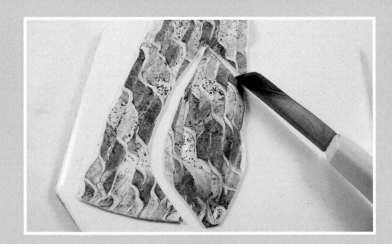

Form a "scrap handle" by shaping a lump of warm, conditioned scrap clay into a ball and pinching the top half to create a handle. Press the scrap handle onto your work surface to flatten the bottom. To make a duplicate shape, roll a smooth 1" (3mm) ball of scrap clay and form it into a football shape. Spritz the mold with water and press the clay into the mold to fill it. Trim the top even with the mold with a slicing blade if needed. Press your scrap handle onto the surface to aid in pulling out the molded clay. Remove the handle slowly and bake the duplicate shape as directed. Allow the clay to cool.

7 Cover the shape with veneer

Apply a thin layer of translucent liquid clay to the shape's surface and drape the veneer over it. Press around the shape gently and cut away excess clay. Press the veneer onto the shape from the inside outward to avoid trapping air between the layers. Press any bubbles towards the edge, or, prick with an extra-fine beading needle and press flat.

8 Trim and bake

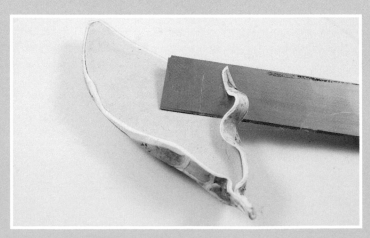

Using a slicing blade placed against the base, trim away the excess veneer clay so it becomes flush with the back side. Roll a white sheet of clay to 1/16" (2mm). I usually add my custom rubber stamped logo to this layer. Apply a thin layer of translucent liquid clay to the backside of the baked shape and press on the white layer for a finished-looking back side.

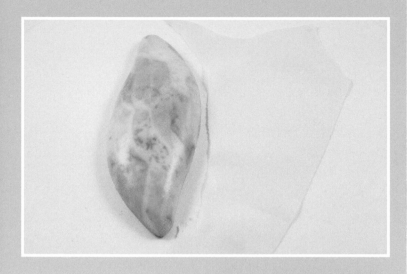

9 Cover with translucent clay

Roll a sheet of frost (bleached translucent) clay as thin as possible (sixth or seventh thickest pasta setting). If the clay becomes sticky during the process, dust both sides with cornstarch or baby powder. Brush away powder. Apply a thin layer of translucent liquid clay to the clay shape surface and secure the thin sheet, pressing from the center outward to push out any air bubbles. Trim off the excess frost clay with a craft blade knife.

10 Sand and carve the design

Using 400-grit and then 600-grit wet/dry sandpaper, sand the clay surface, being careful not to sand too hard or too long in one place. Draw a loose spiral design onto the clay with a grease pencil and then carve over the lines with the linoleum cutter. Carve a shallow channel at first, then go over the same line to create even more depth.

11 Backfill the carved design

Mix a tiny dot of polymer clay softener into three purple clay shades and knead well. Press the soft clay into the carved groove and remove any excess with a paddle-ended tool or the back of your fingernail. Place the colors so they gradually get darker toward the larger area of the spiral design. Add drops of clay softener to a soft cloth and wipe away the clay residue around the spiral design. Bake the piece for 15 minutes and allow the clay to cool.

12 Add the rhinestone and pin back

Using the tip of your craft blade knife, make a cell for the stone by placing it on the clay surface and rotating it around as you dig a tiny hole. Make it just large enough for the stone to sit just above the clay surface. If you wish to sand and buff the piece, refer to the section on finishing on page 21. Glue the point back stone in place with an extra-fine tip of G-S Hypo Cement. Follow instructions on page 31 to secure the pin back.

Organic Bead Bracelet

The surfaces of these bracelet beads are not hard at all to create. You get to use a rubber stamp to create the random-sized and positioned circle shapes and then the chalks do all the work to achieve the fine details. I have listed the chalk colors that I used to make this bracelet, but feel free to change them to your favorite colors. You can use another stamp as well, although I do recommend a bold, geometric design, as it will provide the best results for this technique.

MATERIALS

Ultramarine blue and white polymer clay

Translucent liquid clay

Soft pastel chalk set

Acrylic bead roller

Clear elastic cord

G-S Hypo Cement

Tape measure

Scissors

Soft round paintbrush

1/16" (2mm) drill bit

no. 3 knitting needle (or a wooden skewer)

Masking tape

Rubber stamp (with dots in various sizes)

Cornstarch or baby powder

Ceramic baking

Slicing blade

Craft blade knife

Paper towels

Wet/dry sandpaper

Denim fabric

Potholders

Pasta machine

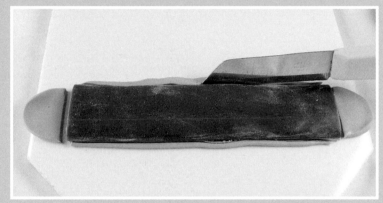

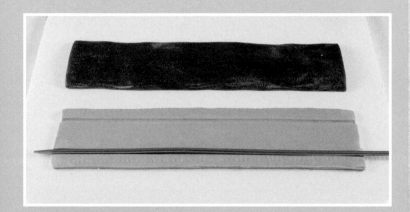

1 Create two domed strips

Roll a rope of blue clay that is ⁷⁄₁₆" (1cm) thick and 10" (25cm) long, and cut it in half. Dust the half oval trough of the acrylic bead roller and the clay ropes with cornstarch or baby powder. Press one rope onto the channel to evenly fill it. Remove the clay and repeat using the second clay rope. Clean powder from the surface with a moist paintbrush. Allow the clay to dry and secure to a ceramic baking tile. Press a stiff slicing blade against the sides of the clay bases to straighten them. Bake for 10 minutes. Allow the clay to cool. Rub a thin layer of translucent liquid clay onto the surface of both strips to act as glue.

2 Form the base

Roll a sheet of blue clay to ⅛" (3mm) thick (thickest pasta setting) and secure to a baking tile. (I have used a lighter blue for clarification; you may use the same blue.) Brush a little water (as a release agent) on the bottom of a strip and set on the blue clay base. Trim the base with a craft blade knife and remove any excess clay. Create a base for the second strip. Remove the domed strips and dry the bottom surface.

3 Create holes for the elastic

Press a knitting needle ¼" (6mm) from each long edge of the bases to create two starter bead holes. Apply a thin layer of liquid clay to the raised area only (not the indentations) of the bases and secure the domed strip tops. Bake for 10 minutes, then allow the clay to cool.

4 Form the veneer

Roll a white sheet of clay through the pasta machine at the thickest setting and secure to a baking ceramic tile. Brush your finger against a stick of periwinkle blue chalk and rub it into the clay surface. Dust the rubber stamp with powder and press firmly onto the clay. Remove the stamp.

5 Decorate the veneer

Rub on random areas of royal blue, purple and fuchsia chalk to the surface using your fingers. Hold each stick of chalk 1" (3mm) above the clay and scrape particles over the clay surface with your fingernail or a craft blade knife. Roll over the clay sheet once with an acrylic bead roller to secure the chalk particles.

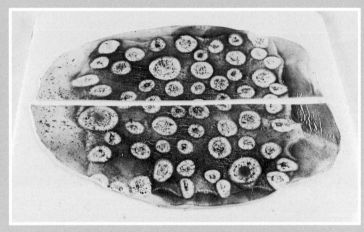

6 Stretch the design

Run the sheet through the pasta machine at the second thickest setting. Wipe the pasta machine rollers with a dry paper towel to remove any chalk residue. Roll the sheet through at the third thickest setting, and then the fourth thickest setting. Clean the roller again. Cut the veneer in half as shown.

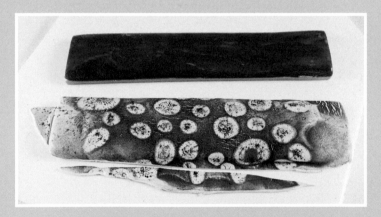

7 Cover the strips

Wet-sand the long side edges and surfaces of each strip until smooth, using 400-grit then 600-grit sandpaper. Let dry. Apply a thin layer of liquid clay to the clay surface as glue. Center and drape a chalked veneer over each strip. Handle the veneer carefully as the chalk can smear at this stage. Trim away any excess clay with a craft blade knife.

8 Trim the veneers

Press the sheet from the center outward to prevent trapping air. Using a slicing blade, trim away the excess clay flush with the bottom edges and the strip ends. Apply a thin layer of liquid clay to the veneer surface and let the project set for 15 minutes. This gives time for the liquid to level itself. Bake for the full recommended time and allow the clay to cool.

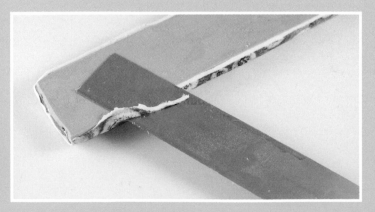

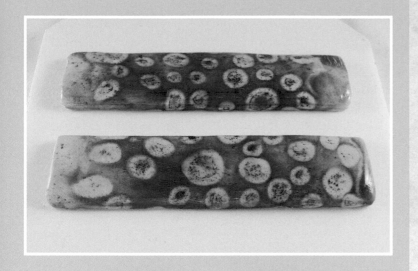

9 Sand and buff the strips

Wet-sand the top and long-side edges of the clay strips (refer to "Finishing" on page 21) starting with 400-grit, working up to 800-grit. Dry the clay strips. Buff the clay surface with denim for a natural sheen. Place one clay strip in the oven for 8 minutes, then remove the tile and place it on a potholder on your work surface. Use a second potholder on top of the tile to prevent your hand from touching it.

10 Cut the strips into beads

The tile will be very hot during this step, so use extreme caution! While the clay is still very warm, slice it into ¼" (6mm) wide beads with a new, sharp slicing blade. Keep the beads lined up and in order. Repeat steps 9 and 10 with the second veneer strip. Measure your wrist. You'll probably have extra beads, so take out the less interesting ones. Cut two 18" (46cm) pieces of clear elastic cord. Fold a piece of masking tape over one end of each cord.

11 String the bracelet

Thread the beads in order onto elastic cord until it is the desired length. If a bead hole is too small, enlarge it with a drill bit while tightly pressing the bead layers together around that hole. Tie the two corresponding ends of each cord together with a square knot. Clip the elastic ends to ⅛" (3mm) long. Add a dot of G-S Hypo Cement to each knot and gently pull the knots into a bead to conceal them.

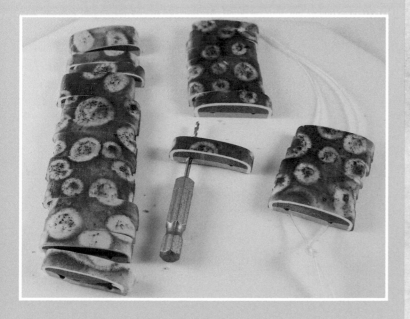

'Chalk Pod' Floral Pendant

This piece is the actual project that I started with, when I first created (well, stumbled upon) my "chalk pod" technique. It can be learned in no time at all. About the time I start thinking that there are no really new techniques, I grab yet another medium from my craft stash and slap it on the clay. Okay, I am exaggerating a bit, but sometimes you just have to try something to see if it will work. And if it does, explore the idea further to see how you far you can push the envelope.

MATERIALS

White, green, yellow, black and
   scrap polymer clay
Soft pastel chalk set
High gloss resin coating
2 smooth ceramic tiles
Premade silver metal clay bail
2-part epoxy
Black 3mm rubber buna cord
Craft blade knife
Paring knife
Acrylic roller
Flexible slicing blade
Wax paper
Small plastic tray
Rubber stamp

TIP

The 'chalk pod' colors lighten up as they are flattened and stretched. Therefore, start out darker then the final desired color, with full, intense chalk coverage on your clay 'palettes.'

TIP

Pastel chalks will act as a semi-release agent when your using the pasta machine to thin the clay. However, when rolling clay through the pasta machine at no. 4 setting or thinner, you'll need to dust the back of the clay with cornstarch or baby powder. Gently wipe powder away with a moist paintbrush before securing it to another piece of clay.

1 Create the chalk palettes

Roll a ¾ cube of white clay to a ⅛" (3mm) thick sheet (thickest pasta setting), cut it into thirds with a craft blade knife and secure two pieces to a ceramic baking tile and one piece to a separate tile. Two pieces will become the palettes. Clean any clay residue from your hands. Rub your finger on a light olive green chalk stick and with a quick motion, tap it onto a clay sheet in random areas. Pick up more chalk and repeat.

2 Add additional color to the palette

Apply hunter green chalk in between the olive colored areas, overlapping some of the olive green spots. If the clay seems to have more hunter green than lime, add some more lime green. Repeat adding chalk colors until there is no white clay showing. Lightly smooth over the colors with your finger. Wash and dry your hands, then create the second chalk palette in the same way, only using fuchsia and purple chalks.

3 Tint the background

Rub your finger over a light turquoise chalk stick and apply an even coat to tint the single white sheet.

4 Form the chalk pods

Using your fingernail, a small scoop or spoon, remove divots of green of clay with a quick motion. Try to pick up some of each green color as well as some white clay.

5 Add the pod-shaped leaves

Make a square indentation around the base to limit the area your flowers will be placed. The design grows a lot as it is stretched and flattened. Arrange the pods onto the clay for the leaves. When you add the flower petals, start by placing 5 to 6 larger pods spaced out from a center point as shown. Overlap the leaf ends when adding flowers.

6 Add the flowers

Secure larger purple pods to create a few more flower bases. Remove some smaller purple divots and secure 4 to 5 petals in between the larger petals. Make sure all of the petals touch other petals so there are no floating petals in the design after it's stretched.

7 Trim the clay edges

Cut out the square and remove the any excess clay. Carefully slide a dull, flexible paring knife under the sheet and lift it from the tile. Roll over your decorated sheet with a clean acrylic roller, once, in both directions to start to flatten the floral pattern.

8 Flatten the sheet

Roll through the pasta machine at the second thickest setting, turn the sheet a quarter turn and roll and the third thickest setting. Turn a quarter turn at roll at the fourth thickest setting. Trim and remove any excess light teal clay from around the shape.

9 Add a white base

Add 1/8 cube of white clay to the light turquoise scrap clay taken from around the project itself (do not use the colored chalk palettes). Condition them together and roll to the third thickest pasta setting. Place the sheet on a tile and secure the floral sheet on top. Roll these two layers through the pasta machine at the second thickest setting. Turn a quarter turn and roll at the third thickest setting and secure on the tile.

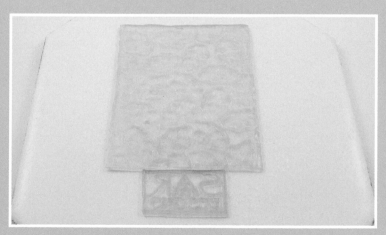

10 Cut the pendant shape

Using your flexible slicing blade, cut the floral pendant shape to have rounded edges. Make it taller than it is wide. This photo shows the side view, as you will turn the tile to work at the top of the shape for each side.

11 Add a green clay mat

Roll a 5/8" (16mm) ball of white clay. Rub light olive and a little hunter green chalk in the palm of your hand and roll the ball between your palms to coat it. Wash and dry your hands. Roll the ball into a 1/8" (3mm) thick rope and secure it around the pendant, cutting the ends at an angle. Press the ends together and smooth the seam. Press the rope flat so it is even with the floral sheet. Cut off the curved edges with a slicing blade, creating a 1/8" (3mm) wide mat.

12 Create the back layer

Remove both chalk palettes from the tile and place on wax paper to re-use for a future project. Secure a rubber stamp to your tile. Roll an extra-large ball of black clay at the second thickest pasta setting. Mist the rubber stamp and press the black sheet onto the clay to texture it. I used my home stamp-making kit to create leaf texture and signature stamps.

13 Add the base

Lift the black clay, secure it to the tile with the texture side down and let it dry. Carefully lift the floral shape and secure it to the black layer. The base must be at least ⅜" (1cm) larger all around. Do not trim the base yet. Roll a ¾" (2cm) ball of clay into a ³⁄₁₆" (5mm) thick rope and secure it around the green mat. Press the clay flat with the pendant. Trim through all layers with the slicing blade to add a ³⁄₁₆" (5mm) wide frame. Bake the pendant as directed for this thickness. Placing it on cardstock for baking will prevent the back from becoming shiny.

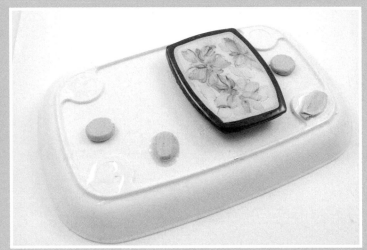

14 Glaze the pendant

Place the pendant onto scrap clay risers that are secured to the back of a small plastic tray. This allows you to slide a stick under the piece to catch any drips that may form. Add a glass-like resin coating to the pendant surface and allow the finish to cure completely. Add a gloss finish such as Future floor finish to the back, and also to the side edges if they are unglazed.

15 Add the bail

When the glaze is dry, glue a pre-made fold-over style silver metal clay bail to the top center edge using 2-part epoxy. Allow enough room for your cord. When the glue is dry and cured, thread the pendant onto the cording of your choice. The sample uses thick buna cord with polymer clay end caps and a magnetic clasp.

VARIATION

This jewelry set is a variation of the project technique using the same pastel chalk colors, only substituting translucent clay for white. There was no clay mat added and the charm with a loop, used as a bail, was pressed into the clay before the final baking cycle.

Love Letters Collage Pin

The art of découpage and layering images together to create a collage has always intrigued me. Most polymer clay transfers are cut into simple geometric shapes. Through trial and error, I discovered a method of cutting through an image and the clay at the same time, making it possible to cut silhouette shapes. The secret is in the heat. Upon removing a project from the oven, I am able to cut through both layers while the clay is still hot and quite soft. Once cool, the transfer becomes permanent and water-resistant.

MATERIALS

White, black and metallic gold polymer clay

Soft pastel chalk set

18-karat gold leafing pen (Krylon)

Gold leaf sheet

18-gauge black vinyl coated Fun Wire (AMACO)

1 7mm round gold jump ring

1 6mm round gold jump ring

1 gold eye pin

1 Swarovski 6mm Padparadscha bicone bead

1 black glass "E" bead

Quick-dry cyanoacrylate glue

E-6000 contact adhesive

Round toothpicks

Shade-Tex Architecture Set shingles plastic rubbing plate

Chinese Noodles Rollagraph stamp wheel (Clearsnap)

Iron-on inkjet T-shirt transfer paper for white or light fabrics (Avery)

Copyright-free image from Dover Publications

Small sharp scissors

Craft blade knife with new no. 11 blade

Flat-nose, needle-nose and round-nose pliers

Three potholders

Ceramic baking tile

Extra-fine mist spray bottle

Pasta machine

Extra-fine mist spray bottle

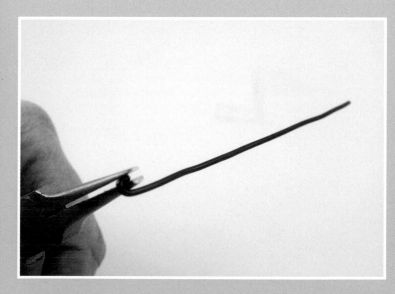

1 Prepare the transfer

Scan the image, then print it using an inkjet printer and Avery-brand transfer paper. (This is the only brand that I've found to work with this technique.) Roll a sheet of white clay on the third thickest pasta setting and secure it to your ceramic baking tile. Cut loosely around the image with scissors, leaving a border of white. Roll the transfer edge toward the center, grasp the top layer and remove the transfer from its paper backing. The image itself is more durable than you might expect.

2 Fuse the image

Press the image face up onto the clay. Burnish with your finger to smooth and secure it to the clay. Cut away and remove any excess clay. Bake for the full, recommended time for the clay brand you are using. Place potholders and the craft blade knife on your work surface so they are ready to use while the clay is hot from the oven.

3 Create the frame

You can work on your wire frame until your clay is ready to come out of the oven, at which time it will need your attention. Cut two 4" (10cm) and two 4½" (11cm) long pieces of 18 gauge black wire. Using flat-nose pliers, grasp a ⅛" (3mm) length on the end of one wire and bend it back on itself to form a small hook.

51

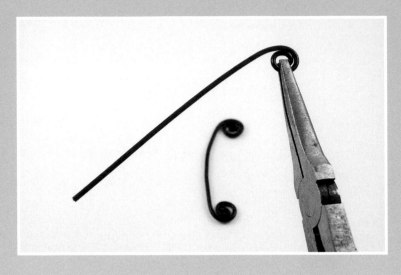

4 Form the spirals

Grasp the hook firmly with flat-nose pliers. Hold the wire in your other hand and bend the wire into a spiral around itself. Continue wrapping until the spiral is approximately $\frac{3}{8}$" (10mm) in diameter. Repeat for all remaining wire ends. Slightly curve the straight area of the wires (refer to step 8).

5 Cut out the images

When finished baking, remove the tile from the oven and place it on a potholder. Do not touch the hot ceramic baking tile or the images. As soon as the images have lost their shine (about 20 to 30 seconds) you may begin cutting. Hold the corner of the ceramic baking tile in place with the second potholder. Lay the third potholder over the bottom of the tile and carefully rest your hand on it. Slowly cut around the images, cutting all the way down through the clay with your craft blade knife. Remove any excess clay when cool.

6 Texture the base

Mix together 4 parts white and 1 part metallic gold clay for the base. Flatten the sheet to the second thickest pasta setting. Mist a rubbing plate with water and secure the clay to the raised, textured side. Run both layers through the pasta machine on the same setting to texture the clay. Peel the clay from the plate and allow the water to dry.

7 Highlight the texture

Rub your finger over rust chalk and apply color to the raised texture on random areas of the clay sheet. Do the same using red, and then yellow-orange chalk.

8 Assemble the frame

Fold your clay sheet in half, back-to-back, so the chalked design is showing on both sides. Flatten the clay to the second thickest pasta setting and secure to a ceramic baking tile. Press the two shorter wires at the top and bottom, and the two longer ones at the sides, curved side in, to form the frame. Run your craft blade knife against the outside of the wire frame to cut away the excess clay. Go back and clean up the clay edges with the blade tip.

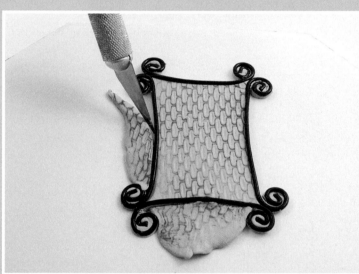

9 Insert the ring

Grasp a 7mm round gold jump ring on the opposite side of the open ends with needle-nose pliers, add a dot of quick-dry cyanoacrylate glue where the ends meet and press halfway into the center of the bottom clay edge. Bake the project for 15 minutes and allow the clay to cool. The wire will be fine in the oven at this low temperature.

10 Outline the images

Run the gold leafing pen along the side edge of the clay images. A thin outline of gold will automatically form around the image itself as the chisel edge curves around it. To reach between tight clay areas, press the leafing pen onto a transfer backing paper scrap, dip a toothpick into the paint puddle and apply to the area. Allow the paint to dry.

11 Secure the images

Secure the letters to the base with E-6000 contact adhesive applied with a toothpick (refer to finished project for placement). Apply adhesive to the back of the silhouette woman, including a small raised dab of adhesive on each wing for support. Secure the silhouette woman to the base. Refer to the main project photo for placement, noticing that the woman's head overlaps the letters. Allow the adhesive to cure overnight.

12 Create the charm

Roll a sheet of black clay to the third thickest setting on the pasta machine and secure a piece of gold leaf to the surface. Smooth out the leaf with your finger. Deeply imprint the surface with a Rollagraph stamp wheel, then cut out a heart shape using a craft blade knife. (You may wish to create extra leafed shapes for future projects at this point.) Remove the excess clay.

13 Add the base and charm loop

Knead and roll the leafed clay scraps to the third thickest pasta setting. Using a craft blade knife, cut a straight top edge. Cut a small "V"-shaped notch out of the center of the top edge. Secure a 6mm gold jump ring with the ends positioned downward, just above the bottom of the notch. Secure the heart over the black clay so the loop is visible beyond the heart and cut away any excess clay around the shape. Smooth the top edges of the heart downward. Bake for 15 minutes. When cool, color the back side of the heart (but not the side edges) with a leafing pen and allow the paint to dry.

14 Add the charm

Follow the instructions for "Beaded Eye Pins" (page 31) to add a 6mm bicone and an "E" bead to a gold eye pin. Open the loops with needle-nose pliers, form a hook and secure a hook into the jump rings to connect the heart charm. Close the loops with pliers. Using the contact adhesive, secure a bar pin back vertically, 1/8" (1mm) from the top center edge of the back of the collage, positioning the pin latch at the top for easy access. Allow the adhesive to cure overnight.

Curved Tile Bracelet

So far this chapter has taught you how to transfer flat images onto polymer clay. That's great, but sometimes you have curved surfaces to work with. I have developed a technique that allows you to fuse an image to a curved surface and tuck the ends in between clay layers to conceal them. The image is transferred in black and white, baked onto the clay and cooled, and then color-tinted with pastel chalks. The bead holes are created automatically as clay strips are placed parallel to each other, with space in between them for the elastic cord.

MATERIALS

Premo! Sculpey polymer clay: white and black

Translucent liquid clay

Iron-on inkjet T-shirt transfer paper for white or light fabrics (Avery)

24" (61cm) long piece of thin, strong elastic cord, either black or clear (must fit into "E" bead holes)

10 black glass "E" beads

Soft pastel chalk sticks

G-S Hypo Cement

Small pointed scissors

Cardstock or 2 index cards

Acrylic bead roller

2 smooth ceramic baking tiles

Round wooden toothpick

Tape measure

Transparent ruler

Extra-fine mist spray bottle

Slicing blade

Small drill bits

Fantastix applicator

Future floor finish

Pasta machine

BRACELET LENGTH

Measure your wrist with a tape measure. Add 1½" (4cm) to the total length so the bracelet will move freely and to compensate for the clasp and "E" beads. From this total length, decide how many 1" (3mm) wide tiles you will need to make.

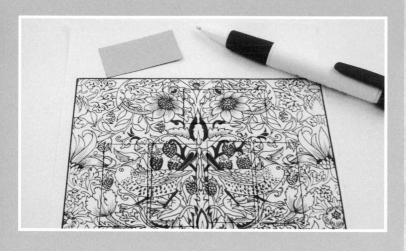

1 Trace and cut the images

Print your image on an inkjet printer using the best quality setting for a borderless photo. Cut out a 1½" (4cm) high by ⅞" (2cm) wide piece of card-stock to use as a template. Trace the template onto the image in 5 to 6 places. Set the image aside to allow the ink to dry and to prevent it from getting wet during the next steps (inkjet ink will bleed if it gets wet at this point).

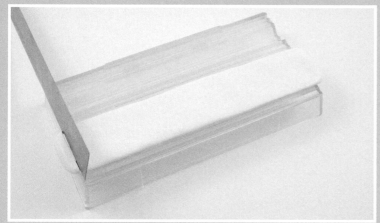

2 Form the beads

Form a smooth ball using ½ cube of white clay. Roll the ball into a ⅝" (2cm) thick by approximately 5" (13cm) long smooth rope of clay. Mist the acrylic bead roller oval trough with water and press the clay rope into the shape. Trim the overlapping ends with your slicing blade. Remove the clay and secure to a ceramic baking tile, flat side down.

3 Cut the beads

Place a transparent ruler up against the side edge of the clay strip. It should measure 5" (13cm) long. If not, trim to this length. Cut the clay into five 1" (3cm) long pieces using a slicing blade. If you're making 6 or 7 tiles, roll a short, ⅝" (2cm) rope, mist the trough with water once again and press rope into the shape. Remove clay strip and cut extra 1" (3cm) long bead(s).

4 Assemble the two-layer bead base

Cut out each image with scissors just inside the traced line. Roll the transfer layer edge toward the center of the image, grasp the top layer and remove the transfer from its paper backing. (The image itself is more durable than you might expect.) Center the image over a clay tile so the rounded edges on are either side and place it onto the clay. Smooth the image, gently rubbing the surface from the center outward and press the top and bottom ends around to the back side of the clay tile.

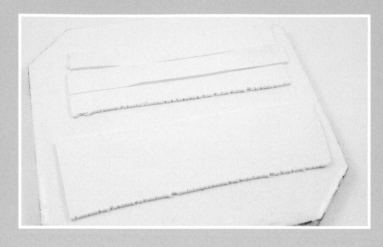

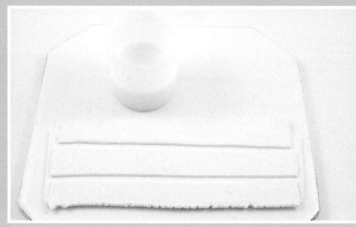

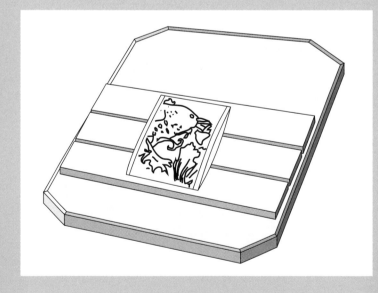

5 Create bottom two bead layers

Roll ½ cube of conditioned white clay to ¹⁄₁₆"
(2mm) thick (third thickest pasta setting), making
a long strip that measures at least 12" (30cm). (If
you're making 6 tiles, make it 14" [36cm]; if 7
tiles, 16" [41cm]). Cut the strip in half and place
pieces on a baking tile. Using a stiff slicing blade,
cut a ⅜" (10mm) wide strip down the center of one
sheet. Lift the ⅜" (10mm) wide clay strip and place
it horizontally in the center of the second sheet. Lift
the remaining two clay pieces and place them on
the second sheet, ³⁄₁₆" (5mm) away from the center
strip, to form two channels (refer to step 7).

6 Assemble the three layer beads

Apply an even coat of translucent liquid clay to
the top strips. Avoid getting the liquid into the
channels. The liquid will act as glue during the
baking cycle to tightly secure the layers together.

7 Cut the base and bake the beads

Press the transfer beads onto the strip, centering
the top and bottom edges over the two channels,
with the curved edges on either side. Cut away
the excess clay from around all four sides of the
beads using a stiff slicing blade. Check the sides
of the beads to make sure the holes will easily ac-
commodate the cording (see a side view of the tile
bead, top right).

8 Form a toggle bead

Roll a smooth ⅝" (2cm) ball of black clay and
shape it so it's tapered at both ends. Pierce two
holes through the bead, ¼" (6mm) apart, using
a toothpick. Place the bead onto a curved index
card or cardstock to bake. Bake all the beads as
directed for the full recommended time for this
thickness of clay. When completely cool, check
to make sure the cording fits through all of the
holes. If needed, you can enlarge the holes with
a slightly larger drill bit. Squeeze the bead layers
together as you slowly drill by hand.

9 Color tint the transfers and varnish the beads

Rub the applicator stick against the side edge of a chalk stick to pick up color, then apply the color inside the designs. You can layer chalk colors as well as overlap them to create blended hues. When the designs are complete, tint the background if desired. I used a fuchsia on the project sample. Tint the remaining white areas of the beads with your background color. Apply 2 or more coats of floor finish to the beads to protect the image and give the tiles a nice shine (refer to "Finishing" on page 21).

10 Assemble the bracelet

Thread 10 glass "E" beads onto the center of the elastic cord. Thread each tile (except the last one), placing one "E" bead between them.

11 Tie off the cording

To add the last tile, thread the elastic through an "E" bead and then through the top hole of tile. Add another "E" bead to the elastic. Thread the elastic up into the right hole of the toggle bead and then down through the left toggle hole. Add an "E" bead and then thread the elastic through the bottom hole of tile. Tie a square knot in the cord ends, add a dot of G-S Hypo Cement to the knot and gently pull it into the second tile bead hole to conceal it.

Etched Leaf Pin

The design featured on this clay pin is created with a piece of paper that has a spiral shape punched out of the center and is cut into a leaf shape. The paper will be pressed onto the clay, acting as a mask, which will prevent the metallic leaf from adhering to this specific area.

This reverse stenciling or "masking" technique is what gives this piece a realistic etched look. Your eye tells you that the black area has been etched or carved away because the metallic leaf appears raised on the clay.

MATERIALS

Black polymer clay

Silver leaf

Piñata alcohol inks: Lime Green, Sunbright Yellow and Sapphire Blue

22-gauge gold wire

1 gold 7mm oval jump ring

1 Swarovski 6mm peridot crystal bicone bead

1 black glass "E" bead

Small spiral craft punch

Fantastix applicators

Wax paper or smooth foil

White coated paper (shiny is best)

Ink pen

Scissors

Acrylic roller

Soft-bristled round brush

Needle-nose pliers

Glass-like resin coating

LEAF PATTERN

1 Create the base

Roll ¼ cube of black clay into a smooth ball. Roll slightly into an oval, then press onto wax paper until it is ¼" (6mm) thick. Punch a spiral out of white coated paper with a spiral craft punch and trace the leaf pattern around it with a pen.

2 Secure the leaf pattern to the clay

Cut out the leaf shape with scissors and press the paper design onto the center of the black clay. Roll over the paper once with an acrylic roller to make sure all the edges are flat and secured well to the clay.

3 Add the silver leaf

Cover the clay with a piece of silver leaf that is slightly larger all around than the pad of clay. Use a soft-bristled brush to smooth the leaf to the clay surface and side edges. Brush away the leaf that is over the paper. Roll the clay over once in each direction to fracture the leaf. Do not remove the paper design.

4 Color the leaf

Carefully drip Green Lime ink over the center area of the clay. Add a few dots of Sunbright Yellow to the center of the spiral leaf design. Let the ink spread out a little. Add drops of Blue Sapphire near the edges of the clay. Add extra drops of color until the surface of the leafed clay is tinted. Try not to use too much ink, use just enough to tint the leaf. The paper design will be saturated with ink, but it won't show on the black clay.

5 Color the side edges

Saturate the pointed end of applicator with Sapphire Blue ink. Add some Lime Green ink to this same tip, and then gently apply ink to the side edges of the leafed clay.

6 Add a jump ring

Allow the ink to set about 5 minutes, then remove the paper design and discard. Grasp a 7mm gold oval jump ring with needle-nose pliers and insert it into the center of the bottom edge of the clay. Bake the piece as directed for this thickness of clay and allow it to cool.

7 Add glaze and the beaded pin

Apply a glass-like resin coating, following the instructions on the package, and allow the piece to completely cure. Form a ¼" (6mm) spiral at one end of a 2" (5cm) piece of 22-gauge gold wire. Thread a crystal bicone bead and then an "E" bead onto the wire. Clip the straight end of the wire to ⅜" (1cm) long and form an eye loop close to the last bead. Refer to "Beaded Eye Pins" on page 31 to add the dangle. Glue a pin back near the top edge of the back of the piece and dry flat.

VARIATION

These earrings are a made in a similar fashion, although after punching the flower out of paper, the paper frame was used instead of the flower shape itself. Cut around the flower hole leaving ½" (1cm) all around to cover the outer black area of the clay. Earring shapes were made with a circle cutter and seed beads were added to the large round jump rings.

Faux Dichroic Glass Necklace

Actual dichroic glass has a thin film of metal (approximately ¼₀th the thickness of a sheet of paper), fused to the surface of the glass, resulting in a metallic reflection that changes between two colors when viewed at different angles. You can replicate this look using metallic leaf that is tinted with alcohol ink. To achieve a glass-like finish on the clay, you will coat it with a two-part resin called EnviroTexLite. You can create fitted, metallic-leafed bezels, which are a type of setting, that will frame your stones with a precious metal look.

MATERIALS

Polymer clay: white, black, translucent, metallic gold, scraps

Translucent liquid clay

Piñata alcohol inks: Baja Blue, Passion Purple, Lime Green, Senorita Magenta and Sunbright Yellow

Silver and gold leaf

Leafing adhesive

20 to 24 Swarovski 2mm sapphire flat back crystal stones

12 (30cm) gold link chain

Gold plated twist clasp

17 gold 7mm oval jump rings

12 gold 6mm oval jump rings

E-6000 contact adhesive or Amazing Goop

Quick-dry cyanoacrylate glue

G-S Hypo Cement

EnviroTexLite pour-on high gloss finish

Small flat brush for adhesive

Fantastix brush-tip applicators

Medium-ball stylus

Double-ended clay tool

Clay extruder

Kemper pattern cutter

Craft blade knife

Wet/dry sandpaper

Ceramic baking tile

Extra-fine mist spray bottle

Cornstarch or baby powder

Needle-nose pliers

Future floor finish

Wire cutters

Pasta machine

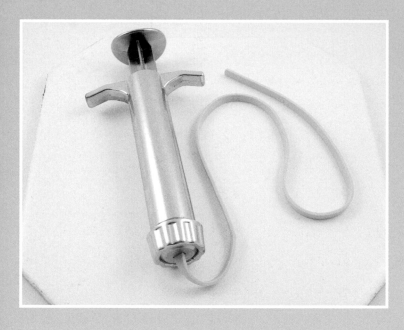

1 Cut six clay strips

Fill a clay extruder with warm, preconditioned scrap clay. Secure the smallest rectangle disc to the end and screw the lid onto the extruder. Extrude a long strand of clay and cut it from the extruder. Using a ruler and a craft knife, cut one each of the following lengths: 1¾" (4cm), 2¼" (6cm), 3" (8cm) , 3⅝" (9cm) and two strands that are 3½" (9cm) long.

2 Form the bezel shapes

Overlap the ends of each strip ¹⁄₁₆" (2mm) and pinch them together to form a joint. Smooth the seams on the top and bottom edges with the flat surface of your fingernail. Shape the 1¾" (4cm) strip into a circle, the 2¼" (6cm) strip into a small oval, the 3" (8cm) strip into a square with rounded corners, the 3⅝" (9cm) strip into a wide oval and one of the 3½" (9cm) strips into a long, narrow oval. Shape the remaining 3½" (9cm) strip into a long, triangle shape that curves to the left, as the shape will be reversed. Bake the clay shapes as directed and let them cool.

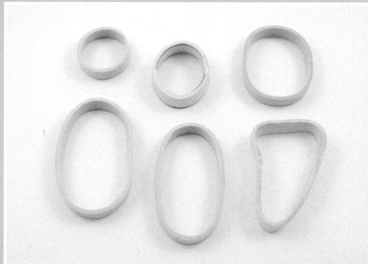

3 Create the bezel molds

Check the frames for any uneven or rough edges and wet-sand them smooth. Roll 4 medium and 2 large balls of conditioned scrap clay. Flatten each onto a ceramic baking tile to form thick pads, for the molds. Make sure that the molds are at least ⅜" (10mm) larger all around than each of the bezel frames. Spritz the clay pads and the original shapes with water. Press the frames halfway down the height of the frame, into the clay and remove the shape. Bake the molds for the full length of time directed for these very thick pieces.

TIP

As all metal clay brands experience some shrinkage when they are fired, it is best create the metal clay piece first and then make the polymer clay piece to fit the bezel.

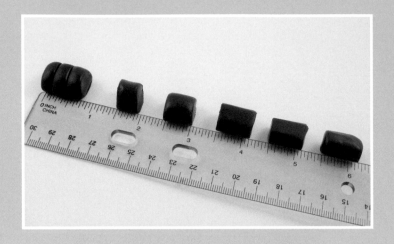

4 Create the stone sizes

Roll a large ball of black clay into a ½" (1cm) thick rope and place on a tile. Cut the rope with your craft knife into the following sized pieces: three ¼" (6mm), one ⅜" (9mm), one ½" (1cm), two ⅝" (16mm) and one ¾" (19mm) long. Roll each into a smooth ball with no visible seams. Keep the balls in this order for reference.

5 Shape the balls

Shape the balls into the basic final shapes, although smaller. Use ¼" (6mm) pieces for 1 round and 2 small ovals, ⅜" (1cm) piece for a slightly larger oval, ½" (12mm) piece for a square, the ⅝" (16mm) pieces for a long thin oval and a large wider oval and the ¾" (19mm) piece for a curved triangle. Do not flatten the bottom sides. Leave the shapes rounded and three-dimensional. Shown in this photo are previously finished pieces so you can relate the size of the rounded black shapes to the finished cabochons for this step.

6 Add leaf to the three shapes

Add a piece of silver leaf to the top surface only of the square, the curved triangle and the long oval clay shapes. Place the tip of the ink bottle on a brush-tip applicator and squeeze to saturate the tip. Dab Lime Green and Sunbright Yellow ink onto the square shape, and just Lime Green on the long oval using the side of the applicator, not the tip. Add Senorita Magenta and Passion Purple ink to the curved triangle. Do not worry if small pieces of leaf come off and onto the applicator. Dab them off onto a folded paper towel and continue applying the ink.

7 Form the veneer and cut the shapes

Roll a sheet of translucent clay to the sixth thickest pasta machine setting. If the clay is sticky, dust one side with cornstarch or baby powder and continue rolling. Secure a sheet of silver leaf to the clay and gently smooth out the surface. Apply patches of inks, overlapping the colors to create blends. Allow the ink to set for 15 minutes, and then cut out small circles with a Kemper pattern cutter and long triangle shapes with the tip of a craft blade knife.

8 Decorate the cabochons

Position the inked cutouts onto the black clay shapes. Turn the shapes over and press the veneered side onto a ceramic baking tile to flatten it somewhat. Flip the shape back over to the front.

9 Shape the cabochons

Place the corresponding original strip bezel frame over the clay to size the cabochon. Remove the frame and make adjustments in the size as needed and smooth the edges of each cabochon. Try to avoid getting fingerprints on the clay surface; if you do, just smooth them out with a light touch with the flat area of your finger. Bake the cabochons as directed for this thickness of clay and allow them to cool.

10 Glaze the cabochons

Following the directions on the package, mix and apply EnviroTexLite to the cabochons. Allow the pieces to fully dry before touching them.

11 Mold the bezels

Roll a sheet of white clay to ⅛" (3mm) thick (thickest pasta machine setting). Mist a mold and both sides of the white clay with water and press the clay into the mold. Press the clay into the mold indentation with your thumb. Slowly lift the white sheet and allow it to dry. Make short clips into the clay edge to flatten. Secure it to a ceramic baking tile and press the cabochon in place.

12 Add texture and decorate the bezels

Cut out a platform around the bezels, leaving room to decorate it with all-over texture. Use a ball stylus tool for dots and the dull edge of a craft blade knife for lines. On the smaller oval (just to the left of the horizontal oval in the project photo), add evenly spaced dots with a medium-ball stylus tool, as stones will be glued into each. Remove the cabochons and bake the bezels as directed.

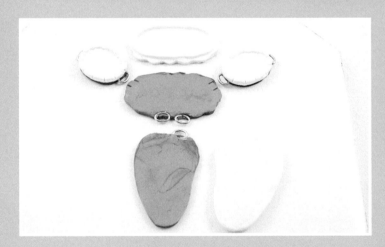

13 Add a base layer and the rings

Roll a sheet of metallic gold clay to 1/16" (2mm) thick (third thickest pasta setting) and secure it to the ceramic baking tile. Mist the back of each bezel to prevent permanent adhesion and place them on the gold clay. Cut the same bezel shape from gold clay using a craft blade knife tip. Remove the bezels. Close the large (7mm) oval jump rings. Holding a jump ring with needle-nose pliers, add a dot of quick-dry cyanoacrylate glue where the ends meet. Press the ring onto the gold base, so it extends halfway off the shape's edge, in the designated positions (refer to step 16 photo). Apply a thin layer of translucent liquid clay to the back of the bezel and secure it to the base. Bake bezels as directed.

14 Add the gold leaf

Apply a thin layer of leafing adhesive to the side edges and the raised rim of each bezel and allow the glue to dry. It will remain sticky. Carefully lay a piece of leaf over the bezel and tamp it down with a soft brush. Apply a coat of Future floor finish over the leaf to seal it, avoiding the center white clay area. Secure the clay cabochons in place using E-6000 contact adhesive and let it dry flat overnight.

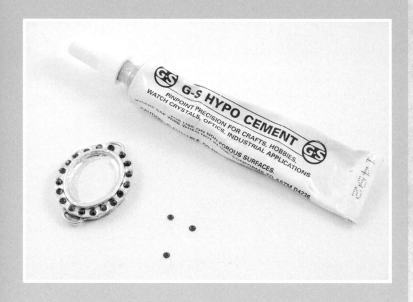

15 Add the crystal stones

Using the precision tip of the G-S Hypo Cement, add a small dot of glue into 3 cells at a time and secure a 2mm crystal stone in place. Use the soft clay end of a double-ended clay tool to pick up and place the stones. Using the baked end of the double-sided clay tool, gently press the stones to set them in place. Allow the adhesive to dry.

16 Assemble the necklace

Open a small (6mm) oval jump ring. Thread it into 2 corresponding bezel rings and close the ring. Secure all bezels together in this manner. Determine your desired necklace length and subtract the length of your clay neckpiece from that measurement. Using wire cutters, snip the necklace chain into 2 even lengths to acquire the desired total length. Secure the chain ends to the last 2 bezels and the clasp loops with jump rings.

Asian Influence Dangles

This is a great beginner project for those who have never added embossing powders to polymer clay. The variegated parchment look on the earring base comes from kneading embossing powders into translucent clay. The color of the clay comes from the powders themselves. Black embossing powder is used to emboss the design onto the surface of the clay and to create an embossed black border around the clay base. A handheld heat gun is needed to emboss the designs. The bead shapes that dangle from the earrings enhance the Asian feel of this jewelry.

MATERIALS

Polymer clay: translucent and red pearl

Embossing powders: black and "Old Paper" Distress (Tim Holtz)

VersaMark clear stamp pad

Translucent liquid clay

4 antique gold 6mm round jump rings

2 antique gold earwires with loop

2 black 8mm round glass beads

2 elongated oval black 10mm glass beads with a vertical hole

Branches with leaves rubber stamp

¼ teaspoon (2ml) measuring spoon

Makin's Clay oval cutter set

Handheld heat gun

Piece of cardstock or large office index card

Make-up applicator

Ceramic baking tile

Craft blade knife

Slicing blade

Needle-nose pliers

Quick-dry cyanoacrylate glue

2 head pins

Pasta machine

1 Mix the powders into the clay

Condition ¼ cube of translucent clay, roll it into a ball and flatten it to a thick pad. Add ¼ teaspoon (2ml) of "Old Paper" distress embossing powder. Fold the clay edges inward around the powder and knead the clay (or roll through the pasta machine) until the speckles are distributed evenly.

2 Cut the shapes and stamp the design

Flatten the clay to a little less than ⅛" (3mm) thick (pasta setting no. 2) and secure it to a ceramic baking tile. Cut out two ovals using an oval cutter and remove the excess clay from around the shapes. Bake the earring bases as directed for this thickness of clay and allow them to cool.

3 Stamp the design

Place an oval on a piece of cardstock that has been folded in half. Stamp the design with the VersaMark ink off to one side of the oval. Sprinkle black embossing powder over the design and allow the excess to fall onto the cardstock. Tap the back side of the clay to allow any excess powder to fall off. Pour the powder back into the jar to reuse. Remove any stray particles with the tip of a make-up applicator (shown in step 4). Heat the design until it becomes slightly raised and shiny using a handheld heat gun. Repeat for the second earring.

4 Emboss the earring edges

Turn the clay over and press the top ridges onto the stamp pad to create a border of ink around the shape. Place on cardstock, clean away any stray powder and emboss as in step 3.

5 Add a bezel

Flatten a sheet of red pearl polymer clay to a little less than 1/16" (2mm) thick (pasta setting no. 4) and place onto a ceramic baking tile. Place an earring face upon the clay and loosely cut around the shape with a craft blade knife leaving a 1/4" (6mm) border all around. Remove any excess clay. Apply a thin layer of translucent liquid clay to the red flange and fold the clay edges up against the earring base.

6 Trim the bezel

Using a slicing blade placed against the earring base, trim away the excess bezel clay so it becomes flush with the stamped oval. Lightly smooth the cut ridge with your fingertip.

7 Add the loops

Close the jump rings with needle-nose pliers. Grasp a ring on the opposite side as the cut ends, add a dot of quick-dry cyanoacrylate glue to the cut-end side, then press the jump ring halfway into the center top edge of the clay, just below the baked layer. Press the back side of the bezel to squeeze the clay around the ring. Secure a second jump ring to the bottom center edge of the clay. Repeat with the second earring and bake the clay as directed for these thicker pieces.

8 Secure the beads and other items

Refer to "Beaded Eye Pins" instructions on page 31 to create two earring dangles using 2 headpins, 2 round beads and 2 elongated oval-shaped beads for the earrings. Open the eye loop, secure the hook into the jump ring at the bottom edge and close the loop with needle-nose pliers. Open the loop of the earwires and attach one to the top jump ring of each earring and close the hooks with the pliers.

VARIATION

You can create this fun necklace using the same techniques you have learned from this project. The largest oval cutter in the set was used for the oval pendant and to cut the football-shaped bead as well. Three jump rings are added to the pendant and two to the bottom edge of the football bead. A horizontal hole runs through the top edge of the football-shaped clay bead. The irregular-cut red rock beads are purchased glass beads strung on nylon-coated beading wire. An antique gold barrel clasp was added to the necklace ends.

Sicilian Spice Bracelet

This link-style bracelet will introduce you to tinted liquid clay with alcohol inks. It is also a good beginner project for carving baked polymer clay. The tool is inexpensive—just a small "V"-shaped linoleum cutter. You can create a custom sheet mold, or carved designs can be backfilled with soft clay (see "Mosaic Lapel Brooch" on page 106).

MATERIALS

Premo! Sculpey polymer clay: white and scrap clay for a mold

Translucent liquid clay

Silver leaf sheets

Leafing adhesive

Piñata alcohol inks: Mantilla Black, Passion Purple, Sapphire Blue, Rainforest Green, Lime Green, Sangria, Calabaza Orange, Tangerine

Silver leafing pen (Krylon)

E-6000 contact adhesive

Soft-lead, white colored pencil

Hard pastel in ivory and black

Speedball no. 1 fine line "V"-shaped linoleum cutter

Soft, old toothbrush

Small circle template or stencil

Soft cloth or dishtowel

Bowl of ice water

Cardstock

Potholder or piece of felt

Extra-fine mist spray bottle

Ceramic baking tile

Craft blade knife

Flat brush

Soft, round paintbrush

Palette

Ball stylus

Paring knife

Future floor finish

Pasta machine

Silver-plated disk and loop bracelet

Two-piece silver plated toggle clasp

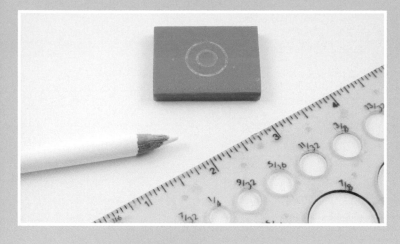

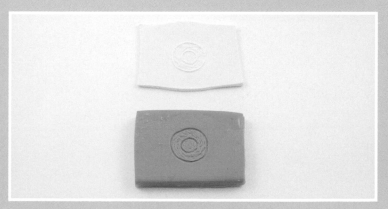

1 Create the slab mold

Flatten a large ball of scrap clay and run it through at the thickest setting on the pasta machine. Cut it in half and stack the two halves so it is a ¼" (6mm) thick slab. Bake the slab on cardstock, according to its thickness, and allow the clay to cool. Using the template and a white colored pencil, draw a ⅝" (16mm) circle on the clay. Draw a ⁵⁄₁₆" (8mm) circle opening inside the larger one, slightly off center.

2 Carve the design

Carve shallow lines with the linoleum cutter, and repeat until the depth is sufficient. Place your clay slab on a potholder or piece of felt and move the clay while carving, instead of your tool, for a smoother cut. This project has an organic look so try not to carve perfect circle shapes. Tip: Later you can use the back side of the slab for another separate mold.

3 Add texture to the mold

To add texture, carve very short, shallow lines, over the inside of both circles. This texture will later give the translucent liquid clay more depth and will reflect the light more effectively once the molded pieces are re-baked. Brush away any loose clay shavings with a soft, old toothbrush.

4 Mold the disks

Roll a sheet of white clay to approximately ³⁄₃₂" (2mm) (third thickest pasta machine setting). Mist both sides of the white clay and the surface of the mold with water. Cut a small square of white clay and press onto the mold. Walk your fingers around the center area of the clay. Lift the clay sheet and secure it well to a ceramic baking tile.

5 Cut out the shapes

Place the tile onto a potholder so you can easily turn the tile while cutting the shapes. Cut around the outside of the raised circle rim, using a craft blade knife. Remove any excess clay. Repeat step 4 to create 10 more disk shapes, misting the mold with water before each use. Cut around each disk. Bake the disks for 10 minutes and allow them to cool. Do not remove the clay from the tile. Leave them adhered to it during steps 6 through 10.

6 Apply the leafing adhesive

Apply a thin even coat of leafing adhesive to the top and side edges of the disks with a flat brush and allow them to dry. This adhesive will become clear and tacky to the touch when dry. Note: Even though metallic leaf will stick to uncured clay, I get a better coverage using adhesive.

7 Add the silver leaf

Carefully cut a 1" (3mm) square of the silver leaf sheet, along with its backing paper. Carefully lift the leaf off the paper with your soft paintbrush and place the leaf onto a disk. Tap it down using the paintbrush to cover the clay. You can add additional small pieces of leaf to any visible white areas, if needed. Use the paintbrush to remove any loose excess leaf. Repeat for remaining disks.

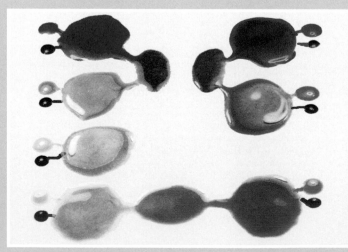

8 Create the colors

Fill 8 wells of a palette halfway with translucent liquid clay. Add one drop of each ink color to a well and mix with a ball stylus tool. Add a small amount of black-tinted translucent liquid clay (not straight ink) to each color in your palette and thoroughly mix. Using only a portion of each muted shade, create 3 additional colors in a separate palette or on a ceramic tile. Mix equal parts of Sapphire Blue with Rainforest Green, Sangria with Passion Purple and Tangerine with Calabaza Orange (shown down the center of the photo).

9 Add the translucent liquid clay and chalk

Scoop up the tinted translucent liquid clay with the ball stylus and allow it to drip into the disk sections. Move the liquid out towards the cell walls with the stylus until the section is full, but not overflowing. Hold a pastel stick 1" (25mm) above each disk and, using your fingernail or a craft blade knife, lightly scrape ivory, then black pastel particles over the liquid clay. The pastel particles add an organic feel as well as a 'salt and pepper' texture.

10 Cure the translucent liquid clay

Bake the disks for a second cycle according to the temperature listed on the liquid clay bottle for the full length of time recommended for this thickness of clay. Remove from the oven and—while pieces are still hot—immediately drop them into a shallow bowl of ice water. Slide a flexible paring knife under the disks to help lift them from the tile when sliding them into the water. When cool, carefully pat the clay dry with a soft cloth or dishtowel.

11 Finish and assemble

Apply metallic paint to the side edges and bottom of the disks with a silver leafing pen. Allow the paint to dry. Apply 1 to 3 coats of Future floor finish to the top and sides of the clay disk edges. When dry, secure a disk to each bracelet pad with the contact adhesive and allow the glue to completely cure. If desired, remove and replace the original fold-over clasp with a toggle clasp, attaching the pieces with oval jump rings.

Champlevé Molded Earrings

It's interesting how many metalworking techniques translate to polymer clay. These earrings, for example, have the look of champlevé, which means "raised plane or field" in French. Traditionally, cells are carved into a metal surface and then filled with enamel. (The results are similar to cloisonné, a technique where tiny metal strips are added to a metal base, forming walls to which enamel is added.) A bi-level polymer clay mold is used to create these earrings and tinted translucent liquid clay is added to the cells to simulate enamel.

MATERIALS

Polymer clay: white and a large amount of scrap clay

Translucent liquid clay

Piñata alcohol inks: Baja Blue, Lime Green, Sapphire Blue and Sangria

2 silver head pins

4 silver triangle bails

2 French-hook earwires with loop

2 Swarovski 6mm amethyst ABB square crystal beads

2 Swarovski 6mm peridot bicone crystal beads

Silver leaf

Leafing adhesive

Clay extruder

No. 0 taper point clay shaper

Bobby pin

Old toothbrush

Fine-line carving tool

Wet/dry sandpaper

Large ball stylus tool

Small ball stylus tool

Ruler

Craft blade knife

Extra-fine mist spray bottle

Ceramic baking tile

Soft-bristled round brush

Palette

Needle-nose pliers

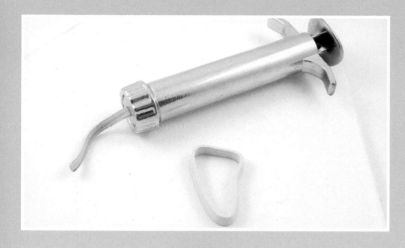

1 Create a bi-level mold

Follow steps 1 and 2 of *Faux Dichroic Necklace* instructions (see page 64) to form a bezel mold from a 3½" (9cm) long extruded strip of clay. Shape it into a triangle that curves. Bake and cool the bezel frame. Check the top and bottom edges of the frame for any uneven or rough spots and wet-sand them smooth. Roll a very large ball of scrap clay into two 1¼" (3cm) balls. Flatten both to create thick pads of clay. Make sure that the clay pads are at least ⅜" (10mm) larger all around than the bezel frame. Press the frames about two-thirds of the way into the clay pads to form two molds, and then remove.

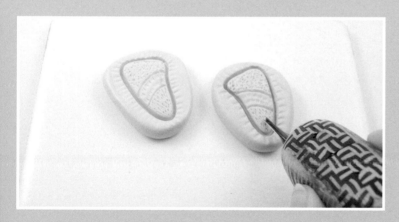

2 Texture the mold

Using the large end of a small ball stylus tool, indent two curved lines in the center of the mold, ⅜" (10mm) apart. Using a clay shaper, add a random dot texture to the top section and lines around the frame spaced ⅛" (3mm) apart. (The lines are added for use in the necklace variation on page 81, but will be cut off for the earrings.) Use the rounded end of a bobby pin to impress markings in the center section.

3 Bake and carve the final texture

Bake the molds as directed for this very thick clay and allow them to cool completely. Carve very short, shallow lines over the bottom sections of each mold using a fine-line carving tool. Brush away any clay shavings with a toothbrush.

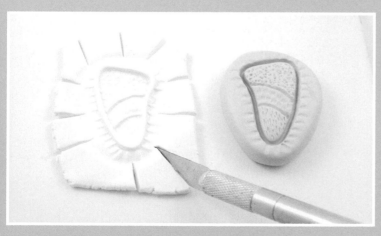

4 Mold two earring shapes

Flatten a sheet of white clay to ⅛" (3mm) thick (thickest pasta setting). Spritz the mold and both sides of the clay sheet with water and press the clay into the mold. Walk your fingers over the clay to press it into the indentations, then remove it from the mold and secure it onto a ceramic baking tile. Cut slits into the edge with a craft blade knife to flatten the clay border. Repeat for the second earring using the second mold.

5 Cut out the earring shapes

Using a craft blade knife, cut around the earring, right up against the raised frame. Bake as directed and allow the clay to cool. (If you want to make the necklace pendant, cut further away from the frame in order to create a detailed, textured rim around the bezel.)

6 Secure loops to earrings

Flatten a white sheet of clay to less than 1/16" (2mm) thick (fourth thickest pasta setting) and secure it to a ceramic baking tile. Place (do not press) the earrings on the white clay sheet, then cut around the shapes with a craft blade knife and remove any excess clay. Remove the baked earring layers and lightly secure two triangle rings to each unbaked section. Place one triangle ring at the top center and one at the bottom tip, with the base of the triangle facing the center of the earring.

7 Add the silver leaf

Apply a coat of leafing adhesive to the surface and side edges of both earrings and allow them to dry. This glue remains tacky once dry. Secure a piece of silver leaf to each, tapping down with a soft-bristled round brush until covered. Clean away any loose leaf by brushing with the soft brush and blowing on the earrings at the same time.

8 Tint the liquid clay and add to the earrings

Fill 4 wells of a palette halfway with translucent liquid clay. Add a drop of ink color to a each well and mix with a small-ball stylus. Add a few dots of the Sapphire Blue-tinted liquid clay to the Sangria-tinted liquid clay to darken it. Using a large-ball stylus, fill each earring cell halfway with Baja Blue-tinted liquid clay. Add the darkened Sangria-tinted liquid clay to the top sections, Lime Green-tinted liquid clay to the center sections and Sapphire Blue-tinted liquid clay to the bottom sections. Tap a small-ball stylus in each cell to partially blend these colors with the Baja Blue-tinted liquid clay. Bake as directed on the liquid clay bottle.

9 Attach the beads and earwires

Follow the instructions on page 31 to create two beaded head pins using the square and bicone beads. Open the loop in the pin, insert into the bottom bail ring and close the loop with needle-nose pliers. Secure the earwires in the same manner.

VARIATION

A necklace can be made with the same techniques as the earrings. There are only a few differences: Mold just one pendant, cutting wider around the bezel before baking. Form two holes near the top corners and bottom center edges instead of using bails, and attach the pendant to a necklace (I chose this crystal-and-silver beaded necklace), add a plated Alacarte twist clasp to the ends and you're done!

Cabochon Ring

The idea of being able to make my own rings has always been exciting. Metal clay is a wonderful medium to use for rings, as it will hold its shape after firing. A variety of different clay, crystal or glass stones can be added to rings. Even though this project is easy for beginners, the results are very elegant. The best part is that when using polymer clay to hold the tiny pointback crystal stones, you do not have to use any glue. Simply press the stones in place and bake.

MATERIALS

White polymer clay

20gm of silver pmc3 (metal clay)

Highly detailed stamp wheel (or rubber stamp)

⁷⁄₁₆" (1cm) circle pattern cutter

Pearl Ex powdered pigments: Sky Blue and Gold Pink

25-30 Swarovski Light Sapphire size PP18 point backed round crystal stones

Soft round paintbrush

Make-up applicator

Rubbing alcohol

Tapered ring mandrel or candle

Small strip of a non-stick craft sheet (or paper) and clear tape

Olive oil

Playing cards

Acrylic roller

Slicing blade

Large-ball stylus

Index card

SIZING A RING

Cut a ¼" (6mm) wide x 3" (8cm) long strip of non-stick craft sheet. Add a small piece of tape hanging over one end. Wrap the strip around your ring finger comfortably, but not tight and secure with tape. Slide the craft sheet ring off and onto a tapered candle. The thickness of the strip and tape will compensate for the shrinkage of the metal clay (pmc3 has only a 12-15% shrinkage rate).

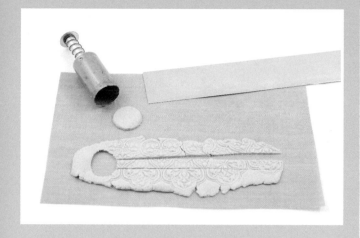

1 Create the bezel base and texture the band

Refer to the "Working With Metal Clay" on pages 26-29 while creating this project. Brush olive oil onto your stamp wheel (or rubber stamp) as a release agent. Roll 12gm of metal clay into a rope and then flatten to a four card thickness (see page 26). Rub a little olive oil onto the clay surface. Cut a 7/16" (1cm) circle and set aside. Roll the stamp wheel over the remaining clay to texture it, pressing down gently. Work as quickly as possible. Cut a 1/8" (3mm) wide strip from the textured clay using a slicing blade. Immediately place extra clay in the original airtight container.

2 Shape the ring band

If you haven't create a paper ring band yet, do it now following the instructions on page 82. Slide a flexible paring knife under your metal clay strip and place it on the paper band. Wrap the strip around the paper and press the ends together. Spritz the clay with water if it's not sticking well to the paper. Smooth the seam, which will later be covered by the bezel. Prop the candle at an angle. You can use a wad of polymer clay to keep it in place.

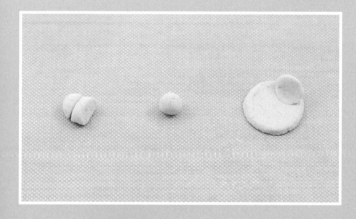

3 Form the bezel

Roll a 1/4" (6mm) ball of metal clay into a 1/8" (3mm) thick log. Cut four 1/16" (2mm) wide slices and place any remaining clay back into the package. Roll each slice into a ball and press it flat like a pancake. Mist the clay circle from Step 1 with water, then secure one of the "pancaked" shapes to the circle, bending this shape up on one edge, then pressing it in place. Add the remaining three "pancakes" in this manner, spacing them evenly around the circle. Use a large-ball stylus to smooth the connecting seams.

4 Add the bezel

Mist the ring connection area with water and press the bezel in place. Use the large ball stylus to smooth the area inside the bezel and to make sure it is well-secured to the ring band. Allow the metal clay to air dry until leather-hard (do not use a heat source with a wax candle). Carefully slide the ring—paper band, clay and all—off the candle and place on a drying rack or screen until it is bone dry. Once dry, place on a firing brick, and using a medium flame, torch the ring. The paper will burn off, but don't worry. Keep the entire ring in the flame. When the entire ring begins to glow pale orange, begin timing. Keep the ring under the flame for 2 minutes. Allow to cool.

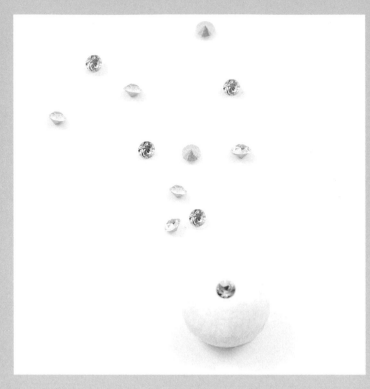

5 Form the cabochon and add the crystals

Roll a ⅜" (1cm) ball of white polymer clay and press onto a baking tile to flatten the bottom. Begin adding stones in the center and work your way toward the cabochon edge. To place the stones, pick them up by gently touching the flat surface of the pointback stones with the uncured tip of a double-ended clay tool. Gently place them onto the clay. Press the stones into the clay using the baked tip of the clay tool, pressing them far enough in that a tiny bit of clay reaches over the top edges of the stone. This way no glue is required. Space the crystals ¹⁄₃₂" (1mm) apart.

6 Secure cabochon into the bezel

Press the cabochon into the bezel and reshape it so that it becomes an even half-round dome shape. The bezel prongs can be positioned either inside or outside of the cabochon. This is your choice. The sample shows the bezel prongs on the outside.

7 Add pigment powder

Pick up some Sky Blue powder from the jar lid with a soft brush. Tap off the excess onto a paper towel, then brush the powder over the cabochon. The powder will stick to the exposed clay areas. Repeat with the Gold Pink powder. When covered, brush the surface vigorously with a clean paintbrush to remove any loose powder from the stones. A make-up applicator tip moistened with rubbing alcohol will clean the stones further. Bake the entire ring on an index card as directed for this thickness of polymer clay. The metal clay is fine in the oven at this temperature.

VARIATION

This ring's band was formed using a clay mold to texture the strip. The millefiori cabochon stone is formed with a cane slice (instructions on pages 111-112 of *Felt Necklace*, steps 1 through 5) that was draped over a clay ball and pressed, pattern-side down, into a round cabochon mold. The metal clay disk was cut with a ½" (12mm) circle pattern cutter that was draped over the back of a plastic ½ teaspoon (2mL) measuring spoon (pictured in on page 95 of *Lots of Dots*, step 5). Once the metal clay was dry, I placed it on 600-grit sand paper and sanded the circle edges flat. This sanded area became the bowl-shaped round 'bezel' for the clay cabochon.

Champlevé Seahorse Necklace

It is so rewarding to create a custom design, make a rubber stamp from the design right at home and then create precious metal jewelry from it. And it's even more fun to wear your jewelry when it's complete, as a true expression of your personal style. With this technique you can imitate the look of Champlevé (shahmp-luh-vay) enamel work by filling the cells of your molded metal clay design with tinted liquid polymer clay. Once the pendant and polymer clay beads are cured, the liquid clay takes on a metallic sheen as the silver metal shows through from beneath.

MATERIALS

White polymer clay

20gm silver pmc3 (metal clay)

Basic metal clay tools (see page 27)

Translucent Liquid Sculpey (TLS)

Piñata alcohol inks: Passion Purple, Sangria, Lime Green, Yellow, Baja Blue and Sapphire Blue

14 sterling silver 3mm beads

7 sterling silver eye pins

4 sterling silver 5mm oval jump rings

14" (36cm) long sterling silver chain (link style)

Sterling silver lobster clasp with loop

AMACO Bead Baking Rack (comes with bead piercing pins, or use wire)

Old, soft toothbrush

Knitting needle or wooden skewer

Small-ball double-ended stylus

Large index card or piece of cardstock

Make-up applicator

Handheld heat tool

9/16" (14mm) oval-shaped pattern cutter

Bowl of ice water

Custom stamp-making kit

Leaf adhesive

Silver leaf

Soft paintbrush

Future floor finish

Nylon-coated pliers

Olive oil

Potholder

1 Mold the design

Use a home stamp-making kit to create the sea-horse stamp, or, if you prefer, purchase a similarly sized stamp to create the mold. Brush olive oil onto the mold, making sure to reach into all of the indentations. Roll a 12-gram lump of pmc3 to a 4-card thickness oval sheet on a ceramic tile. (See page 26). Rub a little olive oil on the clay surface and press clay into the mold. Lift clay and place on tile.

2 Cut out the shape

Cut around the seahorse shape with a lightly oiled craft blade knife, working carefully but quickly. Immediately place the excess clay back into its original airtight container. Use a knitting needle to make a hole $\frac{1}{16}$" (2mm) from the top and bottom center points and allow the project to dry completely. Carefully sand any rough edges or sharp points and wipe away dust.

**SEAHORSE CUSTOM
RUBBER STAMP PATTERN**

If you are creating your own stamp with a home stamp-making kit, use this pattern at actual size. When creating a custom stamp for Champlevé, make sure to reverse the image by flipping it horizontally in your photo program. This way, when you create your "innie" clay mold, your final sheet of metal clay that is pressed into the mold will be facing the correct direction.

87

3 Torch-fire the metal clay

Torch-fire the pendant as directed on page 28-29. The piece will shrink somewhat depending on the brand of metal clay you are using. When the piece is completely cool, burnish the both sides of the pendant with a brass brush.

4 Tint the liquid clay

Fill 6 wells of a palette halfway with liquid clay. Working over a protective surface, add one small drop of ink to each well and stir to tint the liquid. Repeat for each ink color listed. Also, create a small puddle of "plum" tint by mixing together one part Passion Purple-tinted liquid clay with one part Sangria-tinted liquid clay (not straight ink) in a separate well.

5 Begin adding the tinted liquid clay

To apply the liquid clay colors, dip the large end a medium-ball stylus into the liquid and allow it to slowly drip into the cell. At this point just add puddles or 'dots', as the liquid will spread out a little. Do not let the liquid clay rise over the cell walls. If it does, use a make-up applicator to wipe the metal clean. Follow the diagram for color placement.

6 Blend and add additional colors

Blend colors by alternately tapping the two colors shades with a stylus where they meet. One color should graduate into the other. Avoid totally mixing the two colors together. Using the smaller end of the stylus, push the liquid towards the edges and corners of the shapes. Add the additional color 'dots' to the remaining empty cells according to the diagram.

7 Bake the pendant

Blend the last colors by tapping the two colors where they meet. Roll a thin sheet of polymer clay and secure to the baking tile. Carefully lift the pendant and set it onto the clay sheet to prevent it from sliding while carrying it to and from the oven. Bake as directed on the liquid clay bottle. (Metal clay is fine in an oven.) Remove the baking tile from the oven and immediately slide it into a dish of ice water. The cold water will cause the liquid clay to become more transparent. After a minute, remove the piece and dry with a soft cloth.

8 Form the beads

Roll a sheet of white clay to $\frac{1}{16}$" (2mm) thick slab (third thickest pasta setting) and secure to a baking tile. Cut 14 oval shapes with the pattern cutter and remove excess clay. Flip over 7 of the shapes so the smooth side is down. Secure a bead piercing pin (or piece of wire) at an angle across these 7 shapes. Secure a second clay oval, smooth side up, on top of each shape.

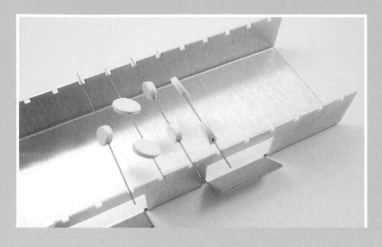

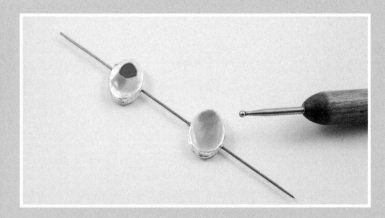

9 Bake the beads

Place the pins on a bead baking rack (or suspend them across lumps of scrap clay) and bake as directed for this thickness. Remove rack from oven, place on a potholder and allow the beads and the tray to cool completely.

10 Add the silver leaf

Do not rotate or remove the beads from the pins. Apply a thin layer of leaf adhesive to the entire surface of the beads, place them back on the rack and allow the glue to dry. It will remain sticky when dry. Carefully secure pieces of leaf over the beads, tapping it down with a soft brush. Make sure the side edges are covered with leaf also. Set the pins with beads on a baking tile.

11 Color tint the beads

Apply a small size puddle of Yellow-, Lime- and Sapphire-tinted liquid clay onto one side of each bead with a stylus tool. Blend the colors randomly so that each bead looks different. Heat the bead surface with a handheld heat tool, held 6" (15cm) from the bead, until the shine turns to a matte fin-ish. This sets the liquid clay. Turn the beads over. Add the same liquid clay colors to the backsides, blend the colors and heat-set. Place the pins back on the bead baking rack and bake as directed on the liquid clay bottle. When finished baking, im-mediately drop the pins with beads into ice water to enhance translucency.

12 Glaze the beads and assemble the necklace

Place the beads back on the Bead Baking Rack. Apply a coat of floor finish and allow the beads to dry. Remove the beads from the wires. If they stick, grasp the wire with nylon-coated pliers and twist the bead until it loosens. Thread beads onto eye pins with a silver bead at each end. Form a loop in the straight end of pins (refer to page 31). Open the eye pin loops, insert into the last chain link and close loop with pliers. Using jump rings, attach the seahorse pendant and the clasp to the necklace chain to complete your project.

VARIATION

This fun neckpiece is made in the same manner as the seahorse. There were three separate metal clay pieces to mold and color with liquid clay. The pieces are connected with silver oval jump rings and a purchased chain necklace with clasp is added to the ends. I simply cut a section of chain out of the center front of the necklace with wire cutters, added jump rings and assembled the neckpiece.

Lots of Dots Charm Bracelet

Many simple shapes can be easily formed with metal clay. By using various textures you can change the look of one shape, a circle for this project, into many styles. This charm bracelet gives the illusion of many metal parts, but in fact, there are only 4 metal clay pieces to form (5 if you count cutting one ball in half). The other silver areas of beads and charms are actually silver leafing. The two mediums blend so well together, that people often think that my leafed bezels, beads and charms are metal!

MATERIALS

Polymer clay: Red Pearl, Cadmium Yellow and White

20gm silver pmc3 (metal clay)

Basic metal clay materials and tools (see page 27)

Silver leaf sheet

Pattern Cutter set; you will use sizes ³⁄₁₆" (5mm), ⁵⁄₁₆" (8mm), ³⁄₈" (11mm), ⁷⁄₁₆" (12mm) and ½" (13mm)

¹⁄₁₆" (2mm) and ⅛" (3mm) diameter small plastic stir straws

9 silver 2" (5cm) long silver headpins

4 silver 5mm round jump rings

2 textured silver 7mm small hole beads

1 silver 4mm small hole bead

Quick-dry cyanoacrylate glue

Double-ended small-ball and medium-ball stylus

½ teaspoon (2mL) plastic half-dome measuring spoon

Soft, round paintbrush

Small sharp-pointed scissors

Needle-nose pliers with cutting area

Round-nose pliers

1 Cut out three charms

Roll a small ball of metal clay on a non-stick sheet, to the thickness of three playing cards and immediately cut out a ⅜" (11mm) and a ⁷⁄₁₆" (12mm) circle with pattern cutters. Cut a ⁵⁄₁₆" (8mm) circle (which will become a separate charm) from the center of the ⁷⁄₁₆" (12mm) circle. Cut one ⅛" (3mm) circle using the straw.

2 Form a ball and add a bail to the donut

Lift the scrap clay from around the shapes and form a ⅜" (1cm) diameter ball. Wrap any extra clay in plastic wrap and place back into the original airtight container. Lift the ⅛" (3mm) circle, moisten the backside and press it onto the open ring charm to use as a bail. Using the straw, imprint circles onto one half of the ball.

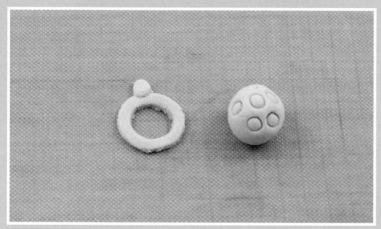

3 Texture remaining half of ball

Turn the ball over. Using a medium-ball stylus, impress dots onto the remaining smooth area of the ball.

4 Cut the ball in half

To create two half-circle cabochons from the ball of textured clay, you'll need to cut the ball in half. Using a slicing blade, gently cut through the ball's center. Allow the ball to rotate while pressing down with the blade to avoid distorting the shape.

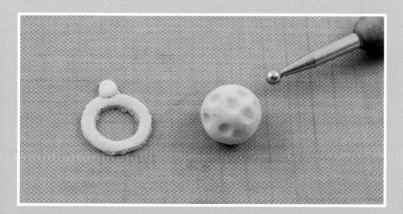

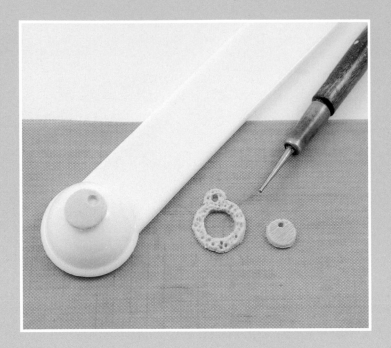

5 Add texture and holes to charms

Pierce a ¹⁄₁₆" (2mm) hole near an edge of the ³⁄₈" (1cm) circle with a small-ball stylus tip and shape the circle onto the dome-shaped measuring spoon. Scratch diagonal lines into the ⁵⁄₁₆" (8mm) circle with the smallest stylus tip and pierce a ¹⁄₁₆" (2mm) hole near the edge with the larger end of the same stylus. Press the stylus all over the ring-style charm randomly to add texture and then pierce a ¹⁄₁₆" (2mm) hole in the bail area. Allow the pieces to air dry completely.

6 Form a color blend and one ball

While your metal clay accents are drying, form a "Skinner Color Blend" as directed on page 24 using cadmium yellow and red pearl clay. Cut off a strip of clay lengthwise with a slicing blade. Slice a ¼" (6mm) strip off the end of the yellow side of the blended sheet. Pinch a tiny amount of red clay from the opposite corner of the strip and thoroughly mix these two colors together. Form a ⁷⁄₁₆" (12mm) size ball using this new yellow-gold blended color. Set aside for step 8.

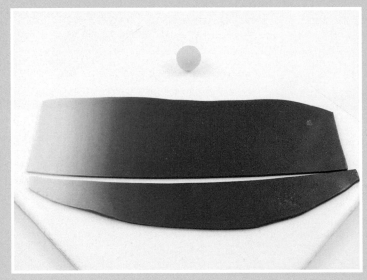

7 Cut out mini dots

Roll the color-blended strip from step 6 to ¹⁄₁₆" (2mm) thick (third thickest pasta machine setting). Make sure the clay is flat and well secured to a baking tile. Using a ¹⁄₁₆" (2mm) diameter straw, cut out several mini-circles from the yellow to red-orange sections. If clay get stuck inside the straw, instead of trying to squeeze it out, simply cut off the straw's tip with scissors. Remove the excess clay strip from around the dots and save it to be used in step 10.

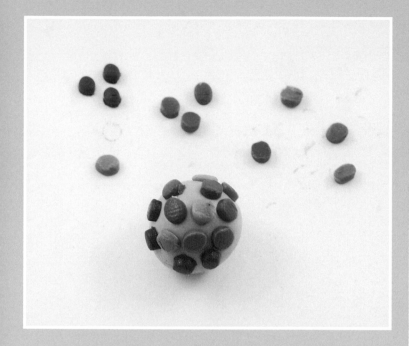

8 Add clay dots

Secure several dots, spacing them approximately ⅟₁₆" (2mm) apart, alternating colors in various positions until the entire ball of yellow-gold clay is covered. Gently roll the ball between the palms of your hands. Do not press them down too hard so that they remain dimensional on the final bead. This will add texture and interest to the bracelet design.

9 Cut and secure small dots

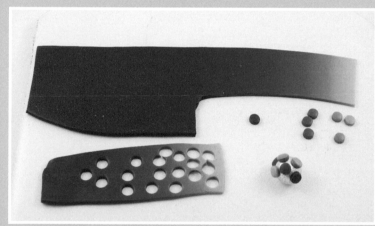

Cut off a small yellow to red-orange strip from the color blend. Do not roll this strip thinner. Using the ³⁄₁₆" (5mm) pattern cutter, cut several dots and save the sheet of clay. Form a ⅜" (1cm) ball of white clay. Cover the ball with silver leaf until no white is showing, tapping down the silver leaf with a soft round paintbrush. To remove any loose, silver-leaf particles, hold the ball with one hand, brush vigorously with the soft brush while blowing strongly on the clay ball. Secure the dots to the clay ball firmly but do not flatten them.

10 Form two additional balls

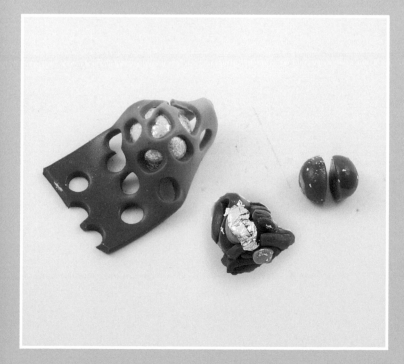

Form a ½" (13mm) ball of white clay. Cover the ball with silver leaf and remove excess loose particles as in the previous step. Wrap the holey sheet of clay from step 9 over the silver ball (at left). Cut away excess clay with small pointed scissors. Gently roll the ball between your palms to smooth the shape. Next, wad up the holey sheet of clay from step 7 (center of photo), place a piece of silver leaf onto the surface and knead the ball together to marble it and to fracture the leaf into tiny specks. Allow the ball to cool from the warmth of your hands for 2-3 minutes and then cut it in half with a slicing blade (at right in photo).

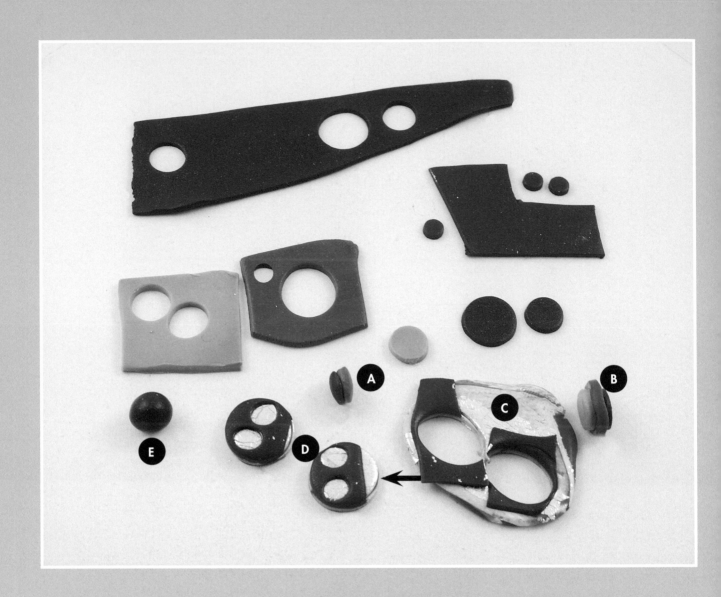

11 Form remaining clay charms

Flatten another strip of the color blend to ¹⁄₁₆" (2mm) thick (third thickest pasta setting). Cut 1 red and 1 orange ⁷⁄₁₆" (12mm) circles, 2 red and 2 yellow-orange ⁵⁄₁₆" (8mm) circles and 1 orange and 4 red-orange ³⁄₁₆" (5mm) circles (save outer scraps of these smallest red-orange circles). Note: you will not use the 3 extra ³⁄₁₆" (5mm) circles, only the sheet of clay that surrounded them. Press together 1 orange and 1 red-orange circle (A). Press a ⁵⁄₁₆" (8mm) yellow-orange and ⁵⁄₁₆" (8mm) red circle on either side of the ⁷⁄₁₆" (12mm) orange circle (B). Flatten some scrap clay with silver leaf to ¹⁄₈" (3mm) thick (thickest pasta setting), then secure 2 square pieces of the red-orange holey sheet to the surface (C) and cut two ½" (13mm) circles (D). Form a ¼" (6mm) red ball (E).

12 Sand the metal clay pieces

When your metal clay pieces are bone dry, gently sand any rough edges with a nail file at this point. Taking a few minutes to clean up your pieces at this stage will make your final silver charms look their best after firing.

13 Torch-fire and burnish the metal clay pieces

Follow the instructions on pages 28-29 to turn your pieces into beautiful fine silver. You may fire both of the cabochons together at the same time, as they are similar in size and weight; fire the three flatter charms in a separate cycle.

14 Add headpins, pierce holes and bake

Press a headpin into all of the round balls until the head is against the bead. The pins will be longer then needed, but wait until after they are baked to clip them shorter. Place a dot of quick-dry cyanoacrylate glue on both sides of bead A (see step 11 photo) and firmly press the metal clay bead halves onto the sides. Pierce a $\frac{1}{32}$" (1mm) hole near the edge in the middle clay layer of bead B with small-ball stylus. Bake all pieces on an index card or cardstock for the full-recommended time for the thickest bead. Metal clay is fine in a home oven.

15 Form jewelry pin loops and attach charms

Clip each headpin with wire cutters so that there is a $\frac{3}{8}$" (1cm) long area beyond the bead. Follow the instructions on page 31 to add a loop to each headpin. Open the jump rings and eye pin loops and secure all beads and charms to the bracelet links, as shown in the diagram.

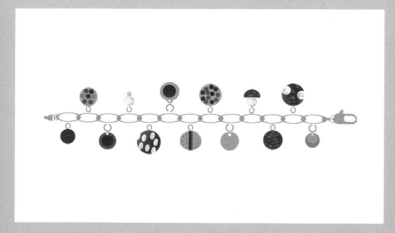

Mosaic Collage Bracelet

The polymer clay mosaic sections of this bracelet may look time consuming, but in fact, all five pieces took only two hours to create. The technique utilizes small strips of clay positioned onto a clay background, which are then impressed with tile lines which create the illusion of separate tiny tesserae. (I was introduced to this strip mosaic technique in a wonderful class I took from Amelia Helm.) To cut the time even further, I have added crystal rhinestones to my collage pieces.

MATERIALS

Polymer clay: White Pearl, Blue Pearl, Red Pearl

5 round 6mm Swarovski crystal AB flatback rhinestones

20 square 4mm Swarovski crystal AB flatback rhinestones

4 Light Amethyst 8mm Swarovski bicone beads

4 Tanzanite 8mm Swarovski bicone beads

Metallic rose seed beads

60 Lime Green ⅛" (3mm) long glass bugle beads

4 Lime Green ¼" (6mm) long glass bugle beads

20 silver 5mm oval jump rings

8 silver 1 long eye pins

Two-part silver toggle clasp

Quick-dry cyanoacrylate glue

Large pointed sewing needle

Double-ended pointed clay tool

Ceramic baking tile

Pasta machine

Craft blade knife

Slicing blade

Needle-nose pliers

COLOR BLEND

Mix the following colors: Rosy pink (8 parts white pearl + 1 part red pearl) and periwinkle (8 parts white pearl + 3 parts blue pearl + 1 part red pearl). Save a little periwinkle to use for the bezel. Create a "Skinner Blend" sheet with these colors (see page 24).

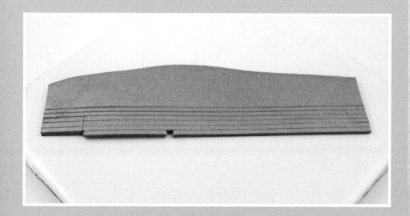

1 Create a round mosaic

Roll a sheet of white pearl clay to approximately $\frac{1}{32}$" (1mm) thick (fourth thickest pasta setting) and secure it to a ceramic baking tile. Pick up and place a 6mm crystal AB stone in the center with the soft clay end of a double-ended pointed clay tool. Press the stone in place with the baked clay end of the pointed clay tool. Thread 2 to 3 metallic rose seed beads at a time onto a large-pointed needle, and slide them off while pressing them into place, just outside the center stone. Position the bead holes left to right, as if they were on a string.

2 Add additional stones and beads

Pick up and press 4 square 4mm Crystal AB stones around the seed beads, spacing them evenly, adjacent to one another. Secure 3 of the small lime green bugle beads onto the needle and press into the clay between each square stone, just outside of the metallic beads.

3 Add the first clay strip

Gradually roll the color-blended clay sheet to less than $\frac{1}{32}$" (1mm) thick (fifth thickest pasta setting) and secure it to a ceramic baking tile. Cut long, $\frac{1}{16}$" (2mm) wide strips across all of the colors. Cut four strips from the periwinkle section, a little longer than the area between two square stones.

4 Create the clay mosaic

Place the periwinkle clay strip against the left edge of a square stone with a craft blade knife. Allow the strip to curve and follow the contour of the glass beads. Gently press the strip in place and cut off the excess against the next square stone with a craft blade knife.

5 Cut the strips into tiles

Using the dull edge of a craft blade knife, cut the strip into ¹⁄₁₆" (2mm) wide tiles. You don't have to cut all the way through the clay. Continue adding periwinkle strips of clay to finish one circle row. (It is especially important that each strip be cut into tiles before adding the next clay strip to avoid unwanted nicks and gouges.) As real mosaic tesserae (tiles) are not usually the same exact color, remove a few tiles and replace them with a slightly different color. Do this for 3 to 4 tiles, but you'll only need to do this for this first circle row; the remaining strips will have color variation from the color blending already.

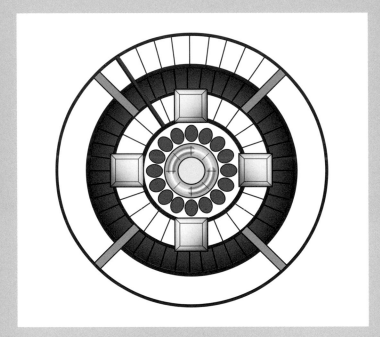

6 Add the longer bugle beads

Using a needle, secure four ¼" (6mm) lime bugle beads centered between the square stones. Cut away a periwinkle-to-lavender section from the color-blended sheet, and place four strips against the first row between the long bugle beads. Cut each strip into tiles before proceeding to the next row.

While you cut the strips into tiles, refer to the adjacent row's cuts: Don't align the cuts, as this will create a "river," or a crack-like dividing line in the design (see diagram).

For the third row, place a lavender-to-rosy pink between two bugle beads strip against the second row, and cut off the excess.

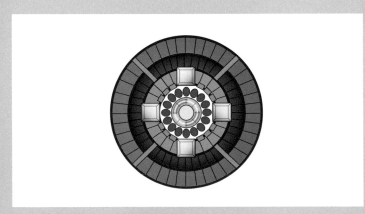

7 Finish adding the clay strips

Add 3 more lavender-to-rosy pink strips against the previous row. Using the craft blade knife, cut around the mosaic and remove the excess pearl background clay. Set project in a safe, undisturbed place while you create the remaining mosaics.

8 Form the remaining mosaic medallions

Follow steps 1 to 6 to create two medium mosaic links (shown left). The design is the same, although you won't add a third row of clay tiles. Also, instead of using the larger, ¼" (6mm) lime green bugle beads as in step 6, add 4 smaller, ⅛" (3mm) lime green bugle beads. To create the two smallest links (shown right), follow steps 2 to 5. The design is the same, although you will use the lavender-to-rosy pink areas of the color blend. Bake all 5 mosaic medallions for 15 minutes and allow them to cool.

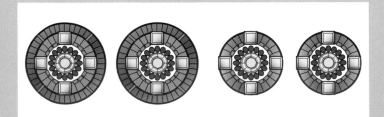

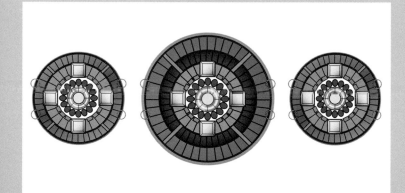

9 Add the clay bezels

To safely lift a mosaic, slide a clean, sharp slicing blade under one edge, keeping the blade almost flat against the tile, and slowly move it back and forth under the piece until it is fully released. Do not bend the mosaic medallions. Roll a sheet of periwinkle clay to the third thickest pasta setting and place on a baking tile. Place mosaics medallions on the periwinkle clay sheet and use a craft blade knife to cut around the shapes, leaving a ⅛" (3mm) flange.

10 Trim the excess clay

Fold up the side edges of the periwinkle clay bases and press them with even pressure against the mosaic edge. Trim away the excess clay by placing a craft blade against the top layer of the baked pieces. Keep the blade almost flat to avoid cutting into the tiles. Lightly smooth the bezel edges with your fingertip.

11 Add loops to the mosaic medallions

Close the jump rings with needle-nose pliers. Position the rings as shown in the diagram. Grasp a jump ring on the side opposite the opening. Add a dot of quick-dry cyanoacrylate glue and press halfway into the side of a bezel, just beneath the baked clay layer. Repeat for the remaining mosaic medallions. On the smallest mosaic medallion, add only one ring where the clasp parts will be added. Bake all mosaics medallions for the full time recommended for this clay thickness and allow them to cool.

12 Assemble the bracelet and add the clasp

Refer to "Beaded Eye Pins" (page 31) to create eight connectors using 8 eye pins, 4 tanzanite and 4 light amethyst bicone beads. Open the loop of an eye pin connector and secure the hook into a mosaic ring. Secure the tanzanite beaded pins to the top row of mosaics and the light amethyst on the bottom row. Close the eye pin hooks with needle-nose pliers. Connect the toggle clasp bar to the single loop of a small clay mosaic and the clasp ring to the other small mosaic medallions with jump rings.

Bird on a Limb

This brooch is assembled on a clear glass sheet so you can follow the pattern beneath. The key to a successful mosaic this small—one with 1/16" (2mm) tiles—is to bake the piece several times, then add new tiles after baking to prevent unwanted nicks and gouges in previously tiled areas. For this project, I created a design with a silhouette of a bird perched on a tree branch and used background colors that resembled a sunset. Any simple pattern will work for this technique, and various brooch shapes will add a different feel.

MATERIALS

Polymer clay: Black, White, Red and Metallic Gold

1" (3cm) gold bar pin back

Quick-dry cyanoacrylate glue

Paper towels

Clear tape

Beveled plate glass sheet

Pasta machine

Liquid softener

600- and 800-grit sandpaper

Buffing wheel or a piece of denim fabric

Craft blade knife

Paddle tool

Slicing blade

BIRD ON A LIMB PATTERN

1 Print and secure the design

Print or trace the bird design. Cut the paper to about 4" (10cm) square and secure face-up under the glass sheet with clear tape. Roll a small ball of black clay to the fifth thickest setting on the pasta machine and place on the glass. Cut the clay into long strips ¹⁄₁₆" (2mm) wide.

2 Begin adding strips to the bird

Add a black strip to the top edge of the bird, allowing the strip to curve along the back and head. Using the dull edge of a craft blade knife, impress each strip into ¹⁄₁₆" (2mm) wide tiles. You do not have to cut all the way through the clay. Continue adding black strips, trimming each to the length of the bird. Impress the lines into each row before proceeding to the next row to avoid gouging nearby tiles. Instead of adding a clay strip for small elements such as the breast area, cut out the rounded shape first, add it to the design and then cut into the tiles.

3 Add the top leaves

Cut out 3 leaf shapes and a thin stem. One at a time, secure them to the design and impress the tile lines. Bake the mosaic for 7 minutes. This hardens the design, making it easier to tile the background without marring the bird tiles. Form a metallic gold to red clay color blend (see "The Skinner Blend" on page 24). Roll to approximately ¹⁄₃₂" (1mm) thick (fifth thickest pasta setting).

4 Tile the background

Secure the color blend to a ceramic baking tile with colors blending from gold on the left to red on the right. Cut the color blend sheet into ¹⁄₁₆" (2mm) wide vertical strips. Take a strip from the center of the color blend sheet and lay it along the bird's back. Trim it so it fits against the left of the top leaf, then impress it into individual tiles. Take a strip from the left side of the blend and add it to the background area, laying it along the previous strip. Impress lines in the tiles, being careful to offset the positions—you don't want to create "rivers" in the design. Continue in this manner until the top section is complete.

5 Continue tiling the mosaic background

Bake for 7 minutes and cool the mosaic. Cut short background strips to fit into the areas between the black tiles. You may create irregular shapes by pressing raw clay on top of the baked tile area and cutting around the embossed shape. Cut angles where needed so strips fit the design. Continue adding strips until the top section is complete.

6 Add the stem and three leaves

Cut a tapered black strip and secure below the bird for the branch, then cut the mosaic tiles. Cut three more leaf shapes, secure them and then cut the tiles. Bake the mosaic for 7 minutes and then allow the clay to cool. Continue tiling the leaves and stems and then the background of the mosaic until complete. Bake the project for an additional 7 minutes and allow the clay to cool.

7 Grout the mosaic

Create "grout" for the tiles by mixing equal parts of white and black clay with 4 to 5 drops of liquid softener. While the clay is warm and pliable, press a thin layer of grout onto the mosaic with your thumb or a paddle tool.

Scrape off the excess grout with the paddle tool, working from the outer edge inward to avoid dislodging the tiles. When most of the grout is removed, there will still be a clay residue on the tiles. Clean a little more off with a few drops of liquid softener on a paper towel.

8 Add the base

Roll a pad of black clay to the second thickest pasta setting and secure it to the ceramic baking tile. Secure mosaic to the base and cut around the shape with a craft blade knife. Bake the project for 15 minutes and allow the clay to cool.

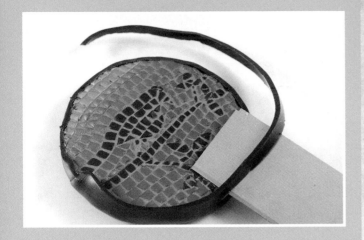

10 Create the frame

Roll the black clay scraps into a long rope and flatten at the fifth thickest pasta setting. Cut a long, ¼" (6mm) wide strip with slicing blade. Using your finger, add a thin layer of liquid softener around the edges and secure the strip. Smooth the seams.

Using a slicing blade, cut off the excess clay to make the frame flush with the top edge of the mosaic. Be careful to avoid the tiles. Bake for 25 minutes and then allow the clay to cool. Carefully wet-sand the brooch with 600- and then 800-grit sandpaper. Dry the clay, then buff on a buffing wheel or with a piece of denim fabric. Glue a pin back horizontally near the top back center edge with quick-dry cyanoacrylate glue and dry flat.

VARIATION

This oval brooch is made with the same techniques as the *Bird on a Limb* brooch. I mixed Pearl White clay into the colors to give the tiles a soft, shimmering effect. This dove design is not a silhouette, so I added a dark beak and eye for extra detail.

105

Mosaic Lapel Brooch

Our final mosaic project is a little different from the previous ones, as you'll be securing the tile strips onto a pre-baked, three-dimensional surface. Your strips of clay will follow the curve provided by the cultured pearl. Your center gem may be a different shape from the sample project, which is perfectly fine! A stone of any shape that can withstand the oven temperature may be used on your vase. Test the stone first by placing it in a preheated oven for 15 minutes. If it comes out undistorted, it's fine to use.

MATERIALS

Polymer clay: Purple, Yellow, White, Ecru and Metallic Gold

Translucent liquid clay

1 small freshwater pearl or stone of your choice

Large-handled paintbrush

Pasta machine

Flexible slicing blade

Paintbrush

Stiff slicing blade

E-6000 contact adhesive

Ceramic baking tile

Cornstarch or baby powder

Craft blade knife

Liquid softener

Paddle tool

Paper towels

Pin back

Cardstock

TIP

As polymer clay can withstand multiple firings (as long as it completely cools in-between), you may decide it is easier to bake the piece after adding each strip, or row. This is fine. Bake the piece for 10 minutes to harden the tiles to avoid gouging them when you are cutting the tiles on the next row. Bake the piece as directed in the following steps to assure a successful project.

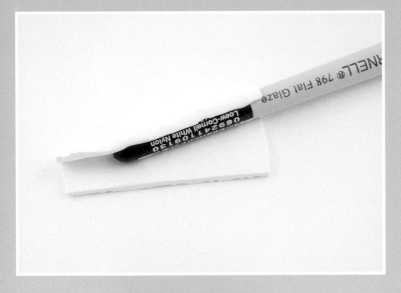

1 Form the vase

Roll a sheet of white clay to slightly thinner than ⅛" (3mm) thick (second thickest pasta machine setting) and secure to your ceramic baking tile. Place the pattern on the clay and cut out the shape with a flexible slicing blade. Dust the paintbrush handle with cornstarch or baby powder, wrap the clay around it and secure the clay edges together. Pinch the bottom narrow end of the vase closed and smooth the corners so they are slightly rounded. Bake the vase as directed for this thickness of clay.

2 Create a Skinner Blend

Form a purple and yellow triangle and blend together as directed in the "Skinner Blend" instructions on page 24. Before running it through the pasta machine, layer a metallic gold sheet of clay on top of the two colors, that is flattened at the no. 3 pasta setting. This will add a metallic gold sheen throughout the blend.

3 Cut narrow strips

Roll the color blend at the fifth thickest pasta setting and cut ⅛" (3mm) wide strips horizontally, across all of the colors, using a stiff slicing blade. Cut a corner off of the lighter end of the first strip, making it tapered. Cut additional strips as needed for the mosaic.

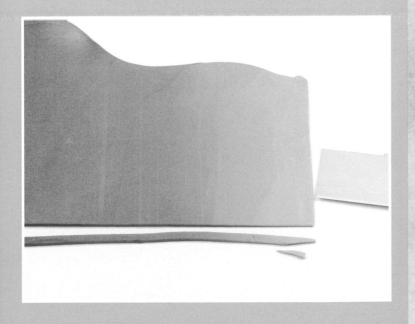

4 Add a pearl

Apply a thin coat of translucent liquid clay to the vase. Secure a small ball of gold clay near the upper right corner. Press a pearl into the gold clay, which will act as a bezel. Smooth the edges of the clay.

5 Secure the first strip

Gently press the tip of the tapered end of the first color strip onto the vase against the bottom of the bezel. Continue pressing the strip, wrapping it around the bezel only once. Allow the clay tail to drape off the vase.

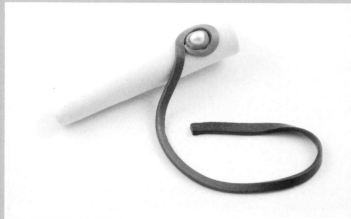

6 Impress the tiles

Using the dull edge of a craft blade knife, cut each strip into ⅛" (3mm) wide tiles. You do not have to cut all the way through the clay, just impress the lines as if you were adding texture. Once the grout is in place they will appear to be separate tiles. Always impress the lines in the rows into tiles before proceeding to the next row to avoid gouging nearby tiles.

7 Add additional strips

Continue to wrap the clay strip around the previous row, impressing tiles as you finish each strip. Re-apply translucent liquid clay as needed. When the clay extends beyond the vase rim, trim it with your craft blade knife so it's even with the edge. When a strip is complete, match the next strip's end color to the previous strip's end color. In other words, if you leave off with plum, start off with plum. This way, the shading will go light to dark and back to light.

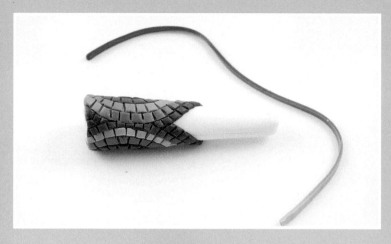

8 Fit the tiles together

When the rows on the back side of the vase are about ⅛" (3mm) from touching each other, stop and bake the vase at the recommended temperature for 10 minutes on a piece of cardstock (to avoid shiny spots on the tiles) and allow the vase to cool. Apply another thin layer of translucent liquid clay to the white areas of the vase. To fit the rows together on the back side, cut a slightly wider strip to fit into the space where needed. Add your next strip and cut it off where it connects on the back of the vase.

9 Tile the vase tip

When the only area left to cover is the bottom tip of the vase, cut short clay strips to fit the area, and impress lines after each one is added.

10 Apply the grout

Create a grout by mixing equal parts of white and ecru clay with 4 to 5 drops of liquid softener. While the clay is warm and pliable, press a thin layer of grout onto the mosaic with your thumb or the paddle tool. Scrape off the excess grout with the paddle tool to clean up the tiles.

11 Clean the tiles

When most of the grout is removed, there will still be a clay residue on the tiles. Add a few drops of liquid softener to a single layer of paper towel and clean the tiles further. Bake the vase for the full time recommended this cycle and allow it to cool. You can wet-sand your vase or leave it as is for a dimensional and textural feel. Secure a pin back vertically near the top edge in the center of the back side with the E-6000 contact adhesive. Lean the vase against a prop if needed, until the glue is dry.

Felt Bead Neckpiece

This project will show you how to create dome-shaped bead caps that are placed up against felt beads. The caps have been lightly textured to give them a matte finish, which enhances the texture of the felt. This is a great beginner project choice for those who have never tried a millefiori cane before. Lots of fun fibers are used to wrap up the neck ring to complete the soft look, giving the piece a touch of whimsy. The felt beads colors you choose will determine the custom clay colors you mix and the fibers colors you add.

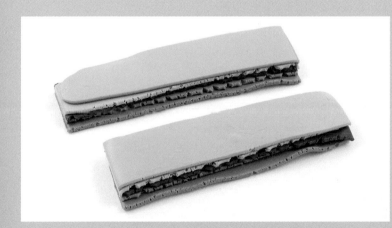

1 Mix the clay colors

Assemble your felt beads on your work surface so you can mix polymer clay colors to match (or co-ordinate) with them. I mixed shades of teal, moss green and a deep blue. The package of hand-made felt beads that I purchased was a coordi-nated mix of cool colors, so it made the necklace color theme a snap!

2 Roll the colors into logs

Place each clay color on your work surface and roll them with the palm of your hand into 2" (5cm) long log or cylinder shapes.

3 Flatten the clay shapes

Flatten each clay log to ⅛" (3mm) thick with pasta machine (thickest pasta setting). Stack the colors in a pleasing manner so a lighter color is next to a darker one, for contrast. Cut the stack in half and place one on top of the other.

4 Create more layers

Cut the stack in half and once again, layer one on top of the other. When you have 20 layers of clay in your loaf, press down on the loaf evenly on all sides with an acrylic roller to condense it and press out any air pockets between the layers.

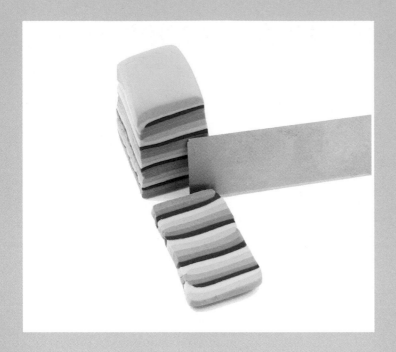

5 Slice the loaf

Using your slicing blade, cut a 3/32" (2mm) thick slice from the clay loaf. Flatten it to 1/16" (2mm) thick (third thickest pasta setting) and secure the slice to a ceramic baking tile.

6 Shape the clay circles

Cut out two 5/8" (6mm) circles using the Kemper pattern cutter and remove any excess clay around the shapes. Repeat this step to create 3 more circles to use as the 5 bead caps. Press a circle onto the back side of the metal measuring spoon to shape it into a dome. Add a light texture to the surface by tapping a stencil brush over the clay.

7 Add a bead hole and heat-set the shapes

Create a hole in the center of the clay dome using a needle tool or toothpick, just large enough to thread the neck wire through. Place the spoon with clay onto a potholder. Heat the bead cap with a handheld heat gun held about 5" (13cm) away from the clay to set up the shape. Fold the sides of the potholder together, pick it up and allow the spoon to gently drop into a bowl of ice water to cool the clay. Carefully lift the clay dome and place it on a ceramic baking tile. Repeat for all 5 bead caps and then bake the caps for the full length suggested for this thickness of clay.

8 Assemble the beads on the neckwire

Pierce a hole in the front center of the felt bead with a needle. Place a bead cap over the hole you've made. Thread a head pin with a silver bead, clip the pin to ½" (13mm) long with wire cutters and place a dot of quick-dry cyanoacrylate glue on the straight area of the pin. Press the pin though the hole of the cap and down into the bead. Unscrew the large silver bead on the neckwire. Thread beads and caps as shown. Add two drops of quick-dry cyanoacrylate glue to the inside of the bead caps and press them against the felt beads. Slide all the beads together and secure the last two silver end beads in place with a drop of quick-dry cyanoacrylate glue placed on the back side of the neckwire.

9 Add the first fiber

Cut fibers to approximately 4" to 6" (10cm to 15cm) long pieces. Tie the first fiber onto the neckwire, right up against a silver bead, leaving a ½" (13mm) tail on one end. Every once in a while, add a dot of quick-dry glue to the underside of the neckwire to keep fibers in place.

10 Continue wrapping the wire with fibers

Hold the fiber tail against and parallel to the wire and wrap the long tail around it several times until it is hidden. Continue adding various colors and texture of fibers to cover the entire neckwire. Fibers can also be tied over existing wrapped areas to have a variation in the thickness of the cording.

Galaxy Bead Bracelet

The controlled swirl of these clay beads is so much fun to create! Moving a bead roller in one direction causes the bead stripes to curve, resulting in the pattern. The gold flecks in the bead are actually a finely fractured layers of gold leaf. The soft wool felt beads are premade, but you will get to customize them by adding small pieces of wool roving. Try to make each felt bead different by placing the roving colors in various areas.

MATERIALS

Polymer clay in colors to match your felt beads

Gold leaf sheets

Strong round clear elastic stretch cord

AMACO Professional Bead Roller Set 4

AMACO Professional Bead Baking Rack with piercing pins

Variety pack of 2cm wool felt beads

10 to 12 gold ⅜" (10mm) diameter disk beads

Small amounts of red, yellow-orange and orchid wool roving

Clover felting brush/mat

Clover Pen-Style Needle Felting Tool

G-S Hypo Cement

Slicing blade

Soft-bristled round brush

Baking rack

Ceramic baking tile

Pin

Future floor finish

Handheld heat gun

Scissors

Pasta machine

114

1 Mix matching colors

Choose three warm felt bead colors and mix three 1½" (4cm) clay balls to match each color. Flatten each to a little less than ⅛" (3mm) thick (pasta setting no. 2) and place on a ceramic baking tile. With a slicing blade, cut off the curved edges, forming rectangles. Save the scraps for step 5.

2 Cover with gold leaf and stack the layers

Cut pieces of gold leaf sheet the same size as the clay slabs. Place the leaf on the clay and tap it down with a soft-bristled round brush. Smooth the surfaces by rubbing over them gently with your finger. Stack the purple sheet onto the red and then the yellow onto the purple sheet. Press together gently to remove any air bubbles.

3 Cut and stack the layers

Slice the clay loaf in half and then cut each side in half again to create four equally wide sections. Stack the four sections together from right to left so you keep the color order the same each time. Press the top of the stack gently to condense the loaf.

4 Cut slices

Allow the loaf to rest and cool for about 3 minutes (longer in warm weather) to become firmer. Using a long slicing blade, trim the side edges and save the scraps. Cut off a ⅛" (3mm) thick slice at a time and gradually flatten it to a little less than 1/16" (2mm) thick (pasta setting no. 4).

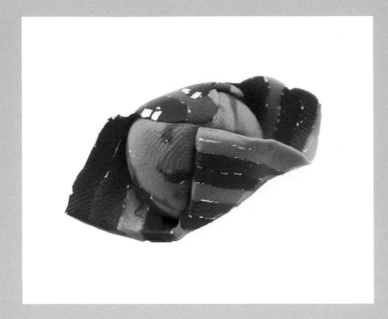

5 Form the beads

Roll six ⁹⁄₁₆" (14mm) size smooth balls of scrap clay for the bead centers. Cut the striped ¹⁄₁₆" (2mm) thick slice (from step 4) in half and wrap two corners around the bead so they meet and touch. Fold the remaining two corner flaps inward in the same manner. Gently roll the clay into a smooth ball with no seams. The ball should measure no more and no less than ⁵⁄₈" (16mm). The size is very important for successful bead roller shapes, so adjust as needed. Repeat steps 4 and 5 for the remaining clay balls.

6 Shape the bead

Place a ball into the larger trough of the bead roller and secure the second half of the roller on top, lining up the same sections. Refer to the tool instructions for this step. Move just the top half of the tool back and forth to shape the bead.

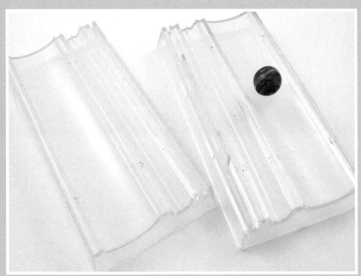

7 Twist and alter the stripes

To twist the bead pattern, this time, do not roll the tool back and forth. Instead, set the bead near the farthest edge of the trough and slide the top part of the tool toward you about 2" (5cm). Repeat— placing the bead near the farthest edge and pulling the top toward you—2 more times. Check the bead pattern and repeat if necessary.

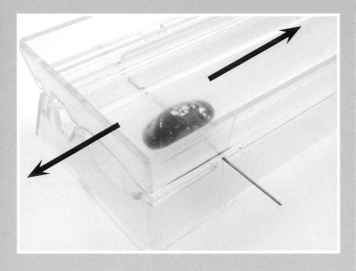

8 Pierce a hole in the beads

Turn the bead so it's parallel with the trough's long edges (shown with arrows), positioning it in the tool so the bead hole placement markings (a vertical line on the side of the tool) are lined up and in the center of the bead. Pierce the bead with a pin by pushing it through the tool opening to the opposite side of the tool. Twisting the pin will aid in piercing the clay. Remove the top half of the bead roller. Lift out the beaded pin and wiggle the pin to enlarge the hole so the stretch cord will to fit through it. Place the beaded pin on a bead baking rack. Repeat steps 6 through 8 for remaining beads.

9 Bake and glaze the beads

Bake the beads on the baking rack as directed for this thickness of clay. Remove from the oven and allow them to partially cool on the rack. While they are still warm, brush on a coat of Future floor finish. Heat them with a handheld heat gun until dry and then repeat adding another coat of floor finish. Reheat and apply a third coat and heat to dry. Allow the finish to cure thoroughly.

10 Decorate the felt beads and string bracelet

Place small pieces of coordinating colors of roving onto random areas of the felt beads. Holding a bead over the felting brush/mat, press the needle felting tool into the bead several times to secure the roving. Repeat for the remaining felt beads. String clay, gold and felt beads onto stretch cord as shown in the finished project photo. Measure around your wrist, adjust the number of beads and then tie a square knot in the cord ends. Trim the ends to 1/8" (3mm) with scissors. Place a drop of G-S Hypo Cement on the knot and pull the knot into a felt bead. Allow the glue to dry.

SECTION
THREE

Gallery

The following pages feature mixed media jewelry pieces created by renowned polymer clay artists. Many of the mediums and techniques can be found in the pages of this book, but each artist has used them in new and creative ways to express their vision. Let their creative work inspire you on your own path.

EXQUISITE MIXED MEDIA

This exquisite necklace was created with sterling silver and polymer clay, strung onto a strand of freshwater pearls. The use of a spiral design is very effective in the piece, becoming both functional and decorative.

untitled pendant
Grace Stokes
Photo by the artist

SIMPLE ELEGANCE

This simply elegant necklace was created using sterling silver, polymer clay and glass beads.

untitled pendant
Grace Stokes
Photo by the artist

MILLEFIORI AND METAL CLAY

This wonderful bracelet uses multiple polymer clay techniques including millefiori canework. The bezels and wirework are sterling silver. The hand-formed elements, textured loop and toggle clasp are made from metal clay and antiqued with liver of sulfur.

Poppy Bracelet
Barbara Sperling
Photo by Robert Diamante

METAL CLAY AND MILLEFIORI

These beautiful bead earrings have incorporated unique, metal clay leaf bead caps, which adorn hand-formed sterling silver wire earring hooks and drops with millefiori polymer clay beads.

Spring Blossoms
Pat Bolgar
Photo by Jerry L. Anthony

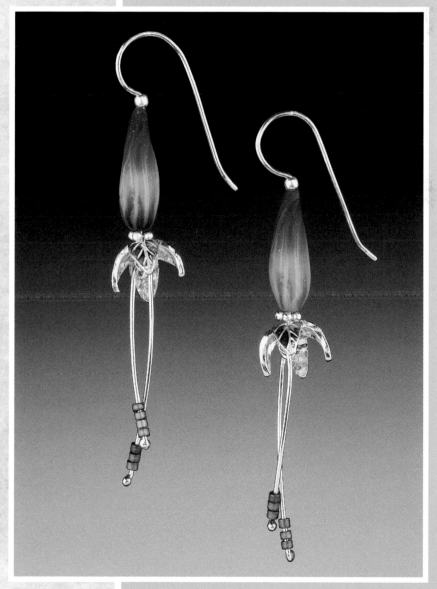

SEMIPRECIOUS

This piece is a beautifully sculpted floral necklace with freshwater pearls, glass beads and semiprecious stones.

Bouquet
Christi Friesen
Photo by Bernard Wolf

GOLD LEAF AND TRANSLUCENT CLAY

This dimensional polymer clay pin includes several mixed media materials and techniques. Kathleen utilizes layers of translucent clay along with gold leaf and her own artwork to create fascinating jewelry designs.

Renaissance Circle Pin
Kathleen Dustin
Photo by Robert Diamante

EMBOSSING POWDER

Mixing embossing powders into various custom clay colors, resulting in a beautiful fall mood to this piece, creates this organic bracelet. Kathleen has placed rubber "O" rings in between each leaf bead allow for the perfect amount of space to be given to each carefully curved leaf. Her bracelet has wonderful movement and texture in the design.

Leaves Bracelet
Kathleen Dustin
Photo by Robert Diamante

MOSAICS

These three brooches include Amelia Helm's mosaic tile application, which she discovered during her experimentation with polymer clay. After taking her workshop and learning how these beautiful mosaics were created, I asked if I could share her technique in my book. She graciously agreed.

Sabre Brooches
Amelia Helm
Photo by the artists

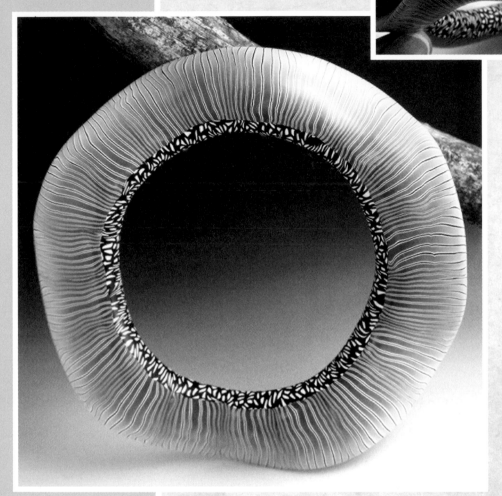

MILLEFIORI

This intriguing bangle bracelet is created with a millefiori technique that mimics actual tree fungi. The armature is partially fabricated to achieve the subtle curves that create movement to the design, which is accented with the precise color placement of the canework.

Wood Fungi BioBangle
Melanie West
Photos by the artist

CLOISONNÉ

This striking necklace is a well-finished and designed jewelry piece with Eugena's signature faux cloisonné technique. Strands of seed beads and freshwater pearls were actually baked into the polymer clay pendant and end caps, allowing for a very clean and flawless finish not possible with any other material but polymer clay.

She, Who Lives in the Trees
Eugena Topina
Photo by the artist

POWDERS

The beauty in these pendants comes to life as Janet carefully applies Pearl Ex powders to shade and highlight her carved and sculpted pieces. They have a very natural look and the fine details are exquisite. She uses paints as an antique medium and finishes with a protective Varathane varnish.

Passionate Heart and Grace Tree Pendants
Janet Wilson
Photo by Shirley Rufener

SCULPTURE

This unique brooch is carefully assembled with the utmost attention to detail. Jeff actually carves the fine lines into the pod bead and then backfills them with other clay colors before re-baking. His assembly and design are always amazing and feature a lot of movement.

Pacific Memoir
Jeff Dever
Photo by Gregory R. Staley

INDEX

TAKE YOUR ART TO NEW LEVELS!

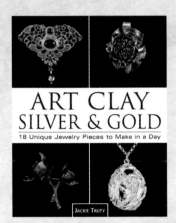

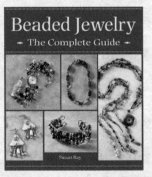
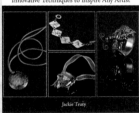